Understanding the New Theology

UNDERSTANDING THE NEW THEOLOGY

CYPRIAN COONEY, O.S.B.

THE BRUCE PUBLISHING COMPANY / *Milwaukee*

IMPRIMI POTEST:

Rt. Rev. Damian Jentges, O.S.B.
Abbot

NIHIL OBSTAT:

John A. Schulien, S.T.D.
Censor librorum

IMPRIMATUR:

✠ William E. Cousins
Archbishop of Milwaukee
July 24, 1968

Library of Congress Catalog Card Number: 68-55278

Copyright © 1969 The Bruce Publishing Company
MADE IN THE UNITED STATES OF AMERICA

IN MEMORY OF MY PARENTS
LEON AND GERTRUDE COONEY
RECENTLY DECEASED

• • •

AGGIORNAMENTO FOUND THEM
IN THEIR EARLY SEVENTIES
AND THEY THOUGHT IT
GREAT

Introduction

This book concentrates on comparing "recent" and "contemporary" theology. One cannot adequately teach theology today without making this comparison. And it seems desirable that it be made in summary fashion in a book devoted to discussing the principal topics of basic theology classes.

With respect to this, the present work may presuppose an undue familiarity with "recent" thought; the burden of its effort is to clarify "contemporary" thought. It may thus have a "simplistic" ring to those in deep admiration of the past. Regarding neither present nor past, however, can this book be of much value apart from further reading, if time for that is available.

By "recent" thought is meant, mainly, the theological understanding that developed and prevailed over the centuries since the sixteenth-century Council of Trent. "Contemporary" thought, on the other hand, refers to the modifications of "recent" thought that have taken place over the past century and a half, and which continue to be responsibly suggested. On occasion, but seldom, "contemporary" thought means a wholly original insight, having little or nothing to do with the theology of recent centuries.

For the most part the book is devoted, with sincere reverence, to tracing the roots of "contemporary" thought in "recent" thought, and to showing how what is "new" fulfills rather than repudiates the "old." The book has no interest at all in presenting mere conclusions; it is devoted to roots, relationships, and organic ties — the stuff out of which genuine theological renewal is forged. By the same token it is wholly absorbed with the greater richness and relevance of "contemporary" theology.

It is this very absorption that makes gratitude to my superior, Abbot Damian Jentges, O.S.B., for permission to write this book so very much in order. His patience in the face of what, on my part, may have appeared to him to be neither "new" nor "thought" has been boundless. Special gratitude is expressed here also to my confrere, Norbert Novak, O.S.B., who consciously and unconsciously lent balance to my thinking time and again. My thanks, too, is extended to Casimir Bernas, O.C.S.O., who generously read the manuscript. To Albert Bauman, O.S.B., former editor of *St. Joseph Magazine*, my indebtedness is altogether special; for his introducing me to writing, for his encouragement and counsel, I am deeply grateful.

And there have been many others — sisters, seminarians, lay students, CCD teachers, adult education participants — whose questions and observations have repeatedly provoked a correcting or clarifying of my thinking. For each of them I am much appreciative. Finally, my sincerest thanks go to all my confreres of Mount Angel Abbey.

This book was written for overworked teachers of CCD and other lay theology classes. It aims simply at facilitating class preparation, its thesis being that it is easier to read fewer than more pages, while doing the thousand and one things that go along with teaching.

For many of the faithful, teachers included, the "new" theology poses any number of problems, not the least being the difficulty of harmonizing the many theological opinions abroad today with the faith of the Church. To some extent the statements of Vatican II, with their non-technical language and emphasis on what unites rather than separates, lessen this difficulty. Pope Paul's *Credo*, of June 30, 1968, however, may well serve to increase this difficulty.

With its insistence on certain technical and traditional ideas this Credo may seem a repudiation of the "new" theology. What has been merely a problem of understanding up to this point may now become a problem of rebuttal. Rather than light, in other words, the "Credo of the People of God" may generate only heat.

Nothing could be farther from the Holy Father's mind, however, than that his Credo be made a "declaration of nullity" regarding the responsible theorizing of contemporary theologians. As he himself professed: "The Church, most assuredly, has always the duty to carry on the effort to study more deeply and to present in a manner ever better adapted to successive generations the unfathomable mysteries of God, rich for all in fruits of salvation."

To be sure, he warned that in this effort "the greatest care must be taken, while fulfilling the indispensable duty of research, to do no injury to the teaching of Christian doctrine." This warning, however, was not in any sense intended as a negative judgment on the research of modern theologians. Neither does the variation between the language or emphasis of his Credo and that of much contemporary theological thinking discredit that thought.

The Holy Father was stating the *faith* of the Church in that form which is and must be both the beginning and testing ground of modern *theology*. He was not doing what theologians do, nor was he doing what he himself as Pope could do, that is, pronounce officially for or against specific contemporary theological opinions.

The problem, then, remains simply what it was before his Credo: striving for understanding and sound theological judgment. To this problem teachers and students of theology today must especially address themselves. Assisting them is the sole aim of this book.

Contents

PART FIVE: Basic Moral Elements

PART SIX: Common Forms of Sin

PART ONE

Signs of the Times

RENEWAL

Meeting of Past and Present

For all that it appears to be wholly exceptional, the present process of renewal in the Church is but a manifestation of the ordinary life of the Church. Surely the Church has gone through renewal experiences before. Had it not, it would have long since disappeared from the scene.

There is, nonetheless, a feature of the miraculous about the Church's renewing itself, both now and in the past. Renewal entails a deep alteration in the thinking and practice of people. And people do not change for the sake of Christ's mission without something akin to a miracle taking place. Participating in the renewal of the Church, therefore, can rightly be said to be participating in the unfolding of a miracle. Cardinal Bea reportedly said as much with respect to the ecumenical movement, and it seems no less true of the Church's overall *aggiornamento*.

Miraculous though it be, renewal remains overwhelmingly a human affair. Beyond the fact that it actually takes place there is little of the extraordinary or stupendous about it. Step by painful step it is worked out by men. It is a process of *their* coming to see new needs, and *their* acknowledging the insufficiency of past achievements.

And as there is nothing particularly dramatic about the process, so there is nothing particularly "new" about what comes to pass. Renewal never takes place in an historical vacuum. It happens, rather, through a process of past things building up to a crisis in the face of a changing situation, and then assuming new forms in response to the challenges of that situation.

Those who see renewal as a sudden, complete, and total leaving aside of the past in favor of wholly new arrangements and attitudes simply fail to see the realities both of past and present. Nothing is happening today that does not have roots in the past, and the present is calling for nothing but a modification of what already is and has long been.

"Renewalists"

There is an eagerness on the part of some to recast things in the Church along completely new, even revolutionary, lines. For a few this involves altering even essentials, though as often as not this implication goes innocently unperceived by them.

For the majority, renewal remains a matter of recasting only accidentals. In their case it is not so much the quality as the scope of their recommendations that calls for tempering. Above all, it is the pace they set for themselves and ask of others that lessens their effectiveness. Both in the realm of doctrine and practice these devotees of "relevancy" urge instant and wholesale alteration of the Church's "face" and "adornments."

One can genuinely sympathize with their objective. One can even suggest that perhaps concern for the Church runs even more deeply in their veins than it does in persons seeking to restrain them. The suspicion which Father Andrew Greeley voiced in his historic article on the "New Breed" in 1964, to the effect that the Holy Spirit will eventually be seen to be with them, seems as sound today as it did then.

Yet, only too often the finest recommendations, the clearest visions of what "could be," even of what "has to be," are presented without any organic connection with what already is. Renewal is conceived as a rewriting of the entire program, as it were, without an eye to the program itself — and especially without an eye to the audience.

It is one thing to sponsor new conclusions, and quite another to work these out in reasonable, convincing form. It is one thing to see possibilities, and quite another to program their achievement. It is one thing to advocate change, even necessary change, and quite another to win support.

Too many "renewalists" are simply not realistically concerned with winning the day. They are not really given to the *total* cause they think they have espoused. Their devotion is to the end in view, but not to the means of its achievement. They would be far more effective, they might even win the war rather than mere battles, if they saw the means of renewal as demanding their main ingenuity and energies.

It is not at all sufficient that in their personal lives or the pastoral niche assigned them they accomplish even consummate relevancy. It is the whole Church that is to be renewed, and the measure of real success is neither the individual nor the group, but the entire community.

Renewalists must begin to think in more wholesome proportions. They must look beyond their immediate surroundings, above all beyond their own particular style of thinking and acting, beyond their own individual "being with it." They must see themselves and their surroundings in relation to the entire Church. One has accomplished very little if one's efforts are paying off only in terms of an individual or "ghetto" installment of renewal. Rather than accomplishment, one may well have produced only "backlash" as far as the Church at large is concerned.

Where renewalists and traditionalists most understandably clash is on the level of "spirit." Open-ended thinking, free-wheeling acting, and above all spontaneous feeling are *subjective*, personal traits, not possessed by all. Call them charisms of the Holy Spirit if you will, they still remain qualities that simply cannot be expected of everyone. And for all their value, for all their necessity in the Church at this time, their possessors can rightly be required to translate their content into forms understandable to those gifted otherwise.

Renewalists, in other words, bear the greater responsibility when it comes to communicating clearly and winning acceptance for their ideas. The principles and experiences that motivate those of a different cast of mind than themselves urge precisely that new and untested ventures, whether of thinking or acting, be studiously avoided by anyone truly seeking the good of the Church. And it is useless to wish these principles and experiences were otherwise, useless too to cite Vatican II as having put the burden of proof on those resisting new ideas. Reality — practical, unavoidable reality — puts the burden of proof, rather, on those advocating practical changes.

The call of the hour, therefore, is for renewalists to be persons of sound methods and intelligent persuasion. Having an idea is not enough. Even less sufficient is having merely a "spirit." One must have scholarship and clarity of presentation. Above all, one must have a commitment to accomplishing renewal. Willingness to "beat the drum," to demonstrate and march, to "bear witness," to protest is not enough. Renewal is not accomplished in the public square or in the spotlight, but in the back room, as it were, where men and women rightly demand of one another solid arguments and intelligent convincing. Until renewalists begin cogently to prove their case, they run the danger of being but "a gong booming or a cymbal clashing."

Doctrinal Renewal

Nowhere is the interplay between past and present more in evidence than in the area of doctrinal renewal. In this area more than elsewhere the renewalist must be skilled at bringing forth "from his storehouse new things as well as old."

Under close examination, the present renewal of doctrine can be seen to be little more than bringing out of the shadows certain features of the orthodox theological tradition which for one reason or another fell out of sight to theologians and the Church. If the renewalist is perceptive enough to know this, and if he takes pains to place his new thought in the framework of the tradition where it belongs, he can not only reduce friction but in all likelihood win needed support. And with support he may well be able to spread his "word" in places where alone he would probably never reach.

A case in point is the person-centeredness advocated today with respect to the celebration of the sacraments. Recent theology dwelt almost exclusively on the sacraments as causing grace apart from the dispositions of the persons participating in them. Based on the teaching of the Council of Trent, this emphasis was a calculated reaction to the Protestant denial of grace-causing power in the sacraments themselves, to the opinion that grace derives from the sacraments solely in virtue of the faith and goodwill of the one(s) receiving them.

The Council of Trent was not denying that the personal dispositions of the participants measure the sanctifying effectiveness of the sacraments. It was simply not saying anything about this, since the situation at hand called for an affirmation that the sacraments are themselves sources of grace.

As a result, though, subsequent theology became concerned almost exclusively with the objective power of the sacraments, and the role of personal dispositions in relation to the fruitfulness of the sacraments was unwittingly minimized. Both in the name of Christ's presence, and for the sake of protecting the faithful from "Protestant" emotionalism, it became customary to teach and celebrate the sacraments in such a way as to keep personal involvement at an unfortunate minimum.

Today, this has all changed considerably. The importance of personal responsiveness and participation is again clearly seen. At least, this is a point made in those documents of the Church which in recent years have looked directly to liturgical renewal.

In many areas of the Church, however, it still remains a problem to convince any number of the faithful, including priests, that the effectiveness of sacraments is only about as good as the personal involvement of minister and participants. Solving this problem requires bringing out of the shadows the traditional theology on the dispositions of the participant as the key to the fruitfulness of the sacraments.

Knowing this traditional doctrine will enable the renewalist to put practical recommendations for liturgical updating on a solid basis. And if he can convincingly state this, his recommendations will have an appearance and impact quite other than "change for the sake of change." His pleading for greater fluidity in the rubrics, for liturgical forms that are adjustable to the age or social level of the participants, for modern music and instrumentation in the liturgy, for modern architecture and church furnishings, will no longer be a novelty, but the very *applying* of the soundest sacramental theology.

A closely related example can be taken from the sphere of law. The theological tradition has always recognized that for a good reason, one which balances the seriousness of the particular law of the Church in question, a person may consider himself excused from that law as long as the reason exists. Illustrations of this teaching, however, have always dealt with causes of an objective kind, like sickness, distance, accidents, duty, etc. Seldom if ever were subjective reasons considered as being suitable even for mentioning, due probably to the desire of avoiding any undue self-centeredness.

The principle at work here, however, does not exclude subjective reasons as suitable excusing causes from Church laws; and the renewalists should not be unmindful of this. Such reasons as personal devotion, the spiritual growth of a person or community, a more pastorally effective sacramental celebration or participation not only come under the traditional principle, but hold, in fact, a certain primacy over more objective and physical reasons. Laws of the Church, after all, aim at personal and spiritual well-being, not at mere physical conformity. Renewal with respect to interpreting excusing causes from laws, therefore, is little more than taking seriously a traditional principle rather than merely its classical illustrations.

A third example deals with doctrine. The tradition has always declared that prudential teachings or directives are not infallible, and can thus change. By force of practice, however, these teachings have customarily been held in such honor as practically to discourage, if not prohibit, the slightest reservation as to their unalterable truth. Identifying prudential teachings, and distinguishing them from infallible teachings, however, is surely one of the *fundamental* roles of theology. Contemporary doctrinal renewal is to a great extent a mere taking of this role seriously, which means little more than applying an aspect of the tradition which for one reason or another was allowed to fall into the shadows.

It means, though, a willingness to "call a spade a spade." If the Church, for example, presents only a prudential judgment regarding the moment when human life begins in the process of human generation, a renewalist will studiously avoid presenting the Church's teaching on abortion in any way that makes the moment-of-conception doctrine appear infallible. Similarly, if the Church has an infallible teaching against contraception, but the scope of that teaching is not altogether certain, a renewalist will insist on due openness with respect to the question of *responsible* contraception as a feature of responsible parenthood. And on these and other issues he will be standing on completely orthodox grounds, even though these grounds may have gone unnoticed in the recent past.

These and countless examples like them serve clearly to indicate that doctrinal renewal is far more a matter of repairing imbalances in the theological tradition than coming up with wholly new ideas. They also illustrate the thorough knowledge of that tradition required of the renewalist if he is at all to be effective.

As for mere procedural changes that have little or no relationship to doctrine, a renewalist can well afford to be less intense and knowledgeable. Such changes are of necessity arbitrary, and can peacefully be left to the discretion of those interested in practical arrangements. An authentic renewalist is concerned only to the point that procedures represent a concrete expression of doctrinal or theological wealth. The actual form of this expression is essentially indifferent, and is wisely not allowed to become a point of wasted energy. A renewalist should be willing to help in the practical arranging of things, but he should know both the limits of his ability and the priority of values involved. To act otherwise is to want merely to talk on the one hand, and to be vain or superficial on the other.

Readings

The Church in Our Day, Pastoral Letter of the American Catholic Bishops (Washington, D. C.: U. S. Catholic Conference, 1968).
Connolly, James, Human History and the Word of God (New York: Macmillan, 1965).
Curran, Charles E., Christian Morality Today (Notre Dame, Ind.: Fides, 1966).
Greeley, Andrew M., "A New Breed," America, May 23, 1964.
———— "The Temptation of the New Breed, America, May 22, 1965.
Houtard, Francois, A Challenge to Change (New York: Sheed & Ward, 1964).
O'Brien, Elmer, S.J. (ed.), Theology in Transition (New York: Herder, 1965).
Rynne, Xavier, Vatican Council II (New York: Farrar, Straus, and Giroux, 1968).
Wolf, Donald J., S.J., and Schall, James V., S.J., Current Trends in Theology (New York: Doubleday, 1965).

PERSONALISM

A Deepening Awareness

Chief among the features of modern man's self-experience is his awareness of himself as a person. This awareness, at least as to its prevalence and impact, has been long in coming. Its origin can be traced through the Romanticism of the nineteenth century to the European Enlightenment of the eighteenth century, and beyond to the Renaissance of the fourteenth and fifteenth centuries.

It is not that man has newly discovered his personal nature. Plato, the Greek philosopher of the fourth century before Christ, first stated that fact for man. And Thomas Aquinas, in the thirteenth century after Christ, added the further clarification that each person is an individual.

No, today it is but a matter of emphasis and implication. With a vengeance, as it were, people are beginning to recognize that as persons they deserve something better than they have been getting — from themselves.

The mood is one of refashioning a situation which right across the board is at all points being found unsatisfactory. Underlying this mood is the realization that human beings are persons. And there is something about that which makes a wholesale change of things imperative.

This blossoming awareness, happily, has not been lost on the Church. At least the major documents of Vatican II took cognizance of it, and one of them, the *Constitution on the Church in the Modern World*, is devoted entirely to it. This, of course, is not to say that all the implications of this richest of Church statements have filtered into every nook and cranny of the ecclesiastical structure. But the Church's message stands in public sight and slowly but surely is leaving its impress.

The Church has acknowledged the correctness of the pervading intuition and has borne solemn witness to its harmony with the gospel. Human beings are persons, Vatican II has said, and for that reason *must* have, both in the Church and in the world, what their personal dignity requires and deserves.

A Matter of Priorities

What does this mean? As far as the Church is concerned, it means what Vatican II meant by conceiving itself as a Council of pastoral renewal. The Church must be *pastoral* in the sense of devoting itself to people rather than to things of ecclesiastical tidiness. And it must be given to *renewal* in the sense of shaping itself to people rather than people to itself.

The principle here is a simple one. As organized powers of service both Church and world exist for the sake of persons, not *vice versa*. Persons, consequently, are to be met "where *they* are," not where the service-structures would like them to be, or even where maybe they should be.

From liturgy to bingo, from foreign aid to postage stamps, Church and world must be person-centered. It is people who must be the basis of policy, not ideals. It is people who must be the basis of problem-solving, not logic. It is people who must be the basis of procedures, not tradition. It is people who must hold primacy in every thought, ambition, effort, success, and failure of Church and world; anything else is betrayal, vanity, and waste.

At the heart of personalism, then, is person-centeredness. It is an attitude of reverence toward both the sameness and uniqueness of human beings. It is an approach to life that takes its signals from real people, an approach that is willing to liquidate anything nonessential to their well-being if such be suggested as a means for achieving their well-being.

It is a mood that cherishes the implicit and ever surprising richness of Pope John's anthem: unity in essentials, freedom in accidentals, and charity in all things. It is a spirit that seeks to release persons from all that does not pertain, while guiding them to what does; and that is concerned and courageous enough to learn and apply the difference.

Personalism is a mind and heart big enough to let rules evolve from people rather than people from rules. It is a perspective that envisions conversation and due compromise rather than intimidation, coercion, or killing. It is a view of life that sets primacy on the law of growth, that is satisfied with steps rather than goals, that anticipates but does not badger the work of grace.

It is a style of life that thrives on honest inquiry, that respects common sense over custom, that expects human issues to be open-ended. It is an impulse that applauds on-the-spot initiative even of an unconventional kind, that refuses to throw the cold water of indifferent convention on matters fundamentally indifferent.

Not a Belittling of God

Personalism is person-centered, nothing else. Karl Rahner means this when he says that love of human persons is implicit love of God, and, by the same token, love of God is implicit love of human persons. Patrick Burke may be right when he writes that there is no love of God except through love of human persons. Surely there is no love at all except that awakened by contact with human persons. Once awakened, though, love — and personalism — can just as surely center directly on God. Yet, what Jesus taught remains ever true: there is no love of God without an attitude of acceptancy toward men — all men. And Piet Schoonenberg definitely gives personalism sure footing when he writes that love is never wholly genuine, whether toward men or God, except through grace, which alone fully opens a person beyond himself in reverence toward God, human persons, and things as they really are.

Person-centeredness is not, therefore, a threat to the primacy of God. It is, rather, a discovery of that primacy, and an acknowledgment of it in the very manner intended by God. As the *Constitution on the Church in the Modern World* makes this point:

> . . . there is a growing awareness of the exalted dignity proper to the human person, since he stands above all things, and his rights and duties are universal and inviolable. . . . God's Spirit, who with a marvelous providence directs the unfolding of time and renews the face of the earth, is not absent from this development. . . . Thus, far from thinking that works produced by man's own talent and energy are in opposition to God's power, and that the rational creature exists as a kind of rival to the Creator, Christians are con-

vinced that the triumphs of the human race are a sign of God's greatness and the flowering of his own mysterious design (26, 34).

To be sure, not any page of the *Constitution* lets the reader forget the deep dependency of man on God, or man's fundamental instability in goodness due to sin. Surely the document avoids all taint of a false "triumphalism" regarding human autonomy and goodness. Just as surely, though, it summons the entire Church, hierarchy and laity alike, to person-centeredness. Moreover, the "triumphalism" it aims specifically to correct is that false complacency which would regard such a summons as unnecessary for the Church. The *Constitution* thought it quite necessary, and in this respect is but a culminating explanation of the changes of thought and procedure called for in other documents of the Council.

The Heart of the Matter

Now, man is not wrong when he regards himself as superior to bodily concerns, and as more than a speck of nature or a nameless constituent of the city of man. For by his interior qualities he outstrips the whole sum of mere things. He finds reinforcement in this profound insight whenever he enters into his own heart. God, who probes the heart, awaits him there. There he discerns his proper destiny beneath the eyes of God. Thus, when man recognizes in himself a spiritual and immortal soul, he is not being mocked by a deceptive fantasy springing from mere physical or social influences. On the contrary, he is getting to the depths of the very truth of the matter (14).

Neither the Council as a whole nor the *Constitution on the Church in the Modern World* was satisfied with a mere summons to person-centeredness. The underlying reason for such a summons was repeatedly stated and inferred. The early chapters of the *Constitution* are in this respect masterful.

The dignity of the human person, as explained in those chapters, follows from man's being an "image of God" as the center and master of creation. This pre-eminence is, in turn, due to man's basic make-up: his body-spirit composition, his mind, his conscience, and his freedom. Ultimately, human dignity consists in sharing Sonship with God in Christ. And what is true of each is even more true of all, since it is in the wholeness of mankind that both "image" and "Sonship" have full and final form.

In perspective and emphasis the *Constitution* is descriptive rather than technical. It hearkens, nonetheless, to technical contemporary thought-patterns, and one finds between its lines abundant testimony to an awareness of current philosophical and theological inquiry into the nature of man. The document also speaks mainly of modern man in general. Countless inferences, however, testify to its attentiveness to the individual person, again in keeping with contemporary interests and inquiries.

As might be expected, the fruit of contemporary reflections on the make-up and life of man is richer and more specific than the generalities endorsed by the Council. Inspired by these reflections personalism is a world view preoccupied with the dignity of persons on the basis of their uniqueness, interiority, and freedom.

Personal Uniqueness

Each person is explained today as called into being (and grace) by a completely singular act of God. Each is a center of identity and possibility wholly unique. No person will ever be reproduced and none can replace another. To each is given an individual version of humanness to bring to fullness, and each is a subject of experiences and relationships never again to be repeated. For each person God and everything in the world takes on a unique and special meaning. And from this meaning is meant to spring a service to which there never has been nor ever will be again an exact likeness.

Personal Interiority

To be a person is also to *stand in being* within oneself. Personal life is interior life, life interior to oneself. A person, therefore, has two sides: one interior, the other exterior. The Council spoke of a person's *body-soul* composition, and in so doing was accommodating itself to a way of thinking that is rapidly being abandoned by contemporary thinkers. Yet even the Council notes that, "Though made of body and soul, man is one." Modern thinkers take this oneness of man most seriously, so seriously, in fact, that they tend no longer to regard man as a being *composed* of soul and body. No longer, for example, is man seen as a being who comes apart, as it were, at death. Rather, man is a being who, while existing permanently within himself, bodies himself forth in a human organism. The human body is thus regarded as the product or form of man's present powers of embodiment. Eventually, with death, and ultimately with glory, greater powers of embodiment will be released. What will ultimately result is a bodying forth in the likeness of the risen Lord.

Personal Freedom

A being of interior self-possession, a person is also by that very fact a being of relationship, of interpersonal self-donation. Standing within himself, a person is called to give himself, to communicate and to share the richness of his own unique mystery. He is to do this with both God and men, and in one and the same process both give and find himself. The power underlying this process is freedom, which has two basic expressions: love and selfishness. A person lives, comes to live, on the basis of choice. As with the individual, so with the community of human persons: they build themselves as persons by freely decided love-interaction, or they stunt and even destroy themselves by freely decided refusal. And always the process, either way, involves time and change: always it can start over, deepen, lessen, or be reversed.

Personalism's Inner Mystery

Theologically speaking, the Council's statement that "God's Spirit . . . is not absent from this development" is of the utmost interest. This implies that personalism pertains either directly or indirectly to the unfolding of God's creative and saving plan. Indirectly, man's increasing awareness of his personal nature is a conditioning for life in the Spirit. Directly, insofar as this awareness is a product of faith, it is itself a sign of man's deepening in the Spirit.

Now grace transforms man: remaining in his humanness, man is by grace enlivened in such a way as to share in the mind and heart of the Spirit of Christ. By grace man is a participant in the very Sonship of Christ with the Father. Within human persons, then, Christ the Son of God is pouring himself forth into humanity, in the case of some by way of conditioning, in the case of others by way of deepening interpersonal union. Each person is thus in some way a projection or extension of Christ in the world. The whole community of men, for its part, is the full expanse of Christ straining to be ever more perfectly present and manifest as the fulfillment of creation's deepest meaning.

At its heart, then, personalism is the most sacred of attitudes, since persons enflesh the Son of God.

Readings

Abbott & Gallagher (eds.), *Pastoral Constitution on the Church in the Modern World*, in *The Documents of Vatican II* (New York: Guild Press, 1966).

Boros, Ladislaus, *The Mystery of Death* (New York: Herder & Herder, 1965).

Burke, Patrick, "God and My Neighbor," *Worship*, March, 1967.

Donceel, Joseph, "Teilhard de Chardin and the Body-Soul Relation," *Thought*, Autumn, 1965, pp. 371–389.

Moral Problems and Christian Personalism, Concilium No. 5 (New York: Paulist Press, 1965).

Nedoncelle, Maurice, *Love and the Person* (New York: Sheed & Ward, 1966).

Rahner, Karl, S.J., *On the Theology of Death* (New York: Herder & Herder, 1961).

———— "The Unity of Love of God and Love of Neighbor," *Theology Digest*, Summer, 1967.

Rogers, Carl, *On Becoming a Person* (Boston: Houghton-Mifflin, 1961).

Schoonenberg, Piet, *Man and Sin* (South Bend, Ind.: University of Notre Dame Press, 1965), pp. 70–79.

Understanding the Signs of the Times, Concilium No. 25 (New York: Paulist Press, 1967).

Van Kaam, Adrian, *The Art of Existential Counseling* (Wilkes-Barre, Pa.: Dimension Books, 1966).

———— *Religion and Personality* (Englewood Cliffs, N. J.: Prentice-Hall, 1964).

Vander Kerken, Libert, S.J., *Loneliness and Love* (New York: Sheed & Ward, 1967).

SECULARISM

Origin of a Tragedy

One of the major misfortunes of history was the Church's inability to respond positively to the Renaissance. Some features of her response were, of course, admirable; others were not.

The Renaissance occurred in the fourteenth and fifteenth centuries. It consisted of the reintroduction into Europe of the cultural products of ancient Greece and Rome, and the recasting of European thought and life according to these. A cultural revolution of the first rank, the Renaissance left no level of European civilization untouched.

The times were ripe for dialogue, and to a certain extent the Church responded creatively. She was especially open to the "new" art, and many classics of Christian art were produced at this time under her influence. Worth noting, though, is that this influence was little more than the "patronizing" activity of certain wealthy families and "worldly" clerics carried on in opposition to the mood and standards of the Church at large.

To the Renaissance as a whole the Church brought only hindsight. It is one of the ironies of history that the very institution which had preserved the pagan classics for Europe was unable to meet their challenge at a later day.

Long in memory, the Church had met these classics before. Her most celebrated intellectuals, centuries earlier, had found them greatly defective as servants of the faith. The influence of their judgment had been to set the Church on an undivided course of "other-worldliness."

The challenge posed by these classics at the Renaissance was two-pronged. On the one hand, they inspired an understanding of man as the center of reality, the very purpose of the world; and on the other, man's own initiative was seen as a source of certain knowledge and mastery of the world. Both impulses — humanism and scientism — threatened a complete reversal of the thought and life prior to that day, the thought and life which for the most part had been of the Church's making.

Had not some small minds in Paris a century earlier won the condemnation of St. Thomas Aquinas — "the greatest of all humanists" — and had not the science of St. Albert the Great — "the most learned man of the whole Middle Ages" — suffered neglect at the same time, the Church might have been much better prepared for the Renaissance. But Thomas, who had "discovered" the individuality of man, and Albert, who was "that rarity indeed, the complete theologian who is also the complete scientist," had been shelved — the climax of three centuries of reactionary conservatism initiated by St. Bernard and consummated by St. Bonaventure.

Church and World Alienated

Unknowingly crippled, the Church recoiled before the Renaissance. What followed is the cultural split known so familiarly today as Church and world: the intellectual and moral division between *ecclesiasticism* and *humanism,* or, in the words of the late John Courtney Murray, between *classicism* and *historical consciousness.*

After the fifteenth century, Church and world went their separate ways. Both developed, both served their self-conceived purposes, and both reaped the fruits, often bitter, of their mutual alienation.

The humanistic and scientific trend quickly featured Machiavelli, Galileo, and Descartes. In steady succession followed nationalism, capitalism, industrialism, and colonialism; Hegel, Nietzsche, and German racism; Marx, Lenin, and communism; Darwin and evolution; Freud and psychoanalysis; James and pragmatism; Sartre and existentialism — in a word, the many elements, including "wars and rumors of wars," that have fused to make the fabric of the modern world.

From this trend has come almost everything typical of modern life in the western world. It has produced the jet and space age, big business and technology, supermarkets and the present standard of living. Its impulse underlies the United Nations, the commanding schools and universities of today, the major literature and entertainment of the times. It has *formed* modern man: his mind, imagination, feelings, and aspirations. It holds daily sway over millions: modern man is in admiration of it, vulnerable to it, even subject to it. He can neither escape it nor awaken desires to resist it. It is the food he eats, the clothes he wears, the fun he has. He loves it.

Meanwhile, back at the Church — Galileo was condemned, Machiavelli abused, Descartes ignored. The Reformation came and went, and with it the unity of Christendom, the Council of Trent adding the final touch to an aborted renewal.

Jesuits and Dominicans bled themselves in an intramural scandal over the complexities of grace and probabilism. In Rome, the Curia vetoed the one real chance the Church might have had to convert the Orient.

Richard Simon was exiled for suggesting that the Bible might mean something other than what it says, and two hundred years later Pere Lagrange, whom Pius XII would eventually honor as the greatest luminary of Catholic biblical scholarship, was distrusted for the same reason.

Evolution was judged ridiculous, socialism condemned, even democracy held in suspicion. The papal states were lost, and Pius IX began his historic "pout" in protest.

The condemnations associated with Vatican I and the later decree against Modernism all but squelched high-level intellectual life among Catholics. The Index of Forbidden Books grew steadily in length. Newman's conversion was doubted, and a budding ecumenical movement, step by step, was thwarted.

As late as the mid-twentieth century, scholars the like of John Courtney Murray and Stanislaus Lyonnet were silenced, and "periti" the caliber of Karl Rahner and Henri de Lubac were thought latter-day Modernists. With their vindication, Teilhard de Chardin, whose "futuristic" *suggestions* presuppose a living theology for their just criticism, became the next target.

The scene was one of depressing introversion and defensiveness, a paralysis of "creeping infallibility" steadily sucking away the creativeness of the Church, closing it ever more forcibly against the world around it. For all that it listed giants of culture and science in its ranks, and for all that it invariably claimed good reasons for its decisions, by the time of Vatican Council II the Church had become a monumental bore.

Such, at least, it was in relation to the world. With respect to itself, it had become, at best, a pseudo-world, possessed of a total culture of its own, including a legal and moral system, a language, a pageantry of festivals and status distinctions. Worst of all, it possessed a body of knowledge which both in the name of reason and the gospel solidified hierarchy and laity alike in an unbending isolationism.

Bridging the Gap

Between the lines of Vatican II's *Constitution on the Church in the Modern World*, then, one is to see a very sour situation begging for urgent and decisive cure. It was the regrettable gap between Church and world that made this *Constitution* at once the finest and most difficult achievement of the Council.

With that document and the theologizing it has inspired, the Church has at this time put its finger on one of the very soft spots in its traditional theology, namely, the relationship between Christians and the world. Theologians today are seriously beginning to ask whether the traditional explanation of this relationship is really accurate or merely a covering for an embarrassing situation.

They have not as yet answered this question. Their discussions, however, clearly show the direction they are taking in search of an answer. Three things are receiving special attention: the meaning of the world in itself, even apart from the Church; the unfolding of God's saving plan in the world as well as in the Church; and the lessening of *ecclesiasticism* in the Church for the sake of a richer and more meaningful contribution to the world.

Of these three things the first, implying as it does a notion of *continuing creation*, and the second, being a feature of contemporary theology's broader understanding of the workings of divine grace, will be treated later, under the headings *Process* and *Grace*. The third will be treated here under the widely accepted heading of "Christian Secularism."

Christian Secularism

Many Christian writers today speak of an honorable secularism.

This is not a little surprising, since several decades ago secularism was thought the greatest modern threat to Christianity. At the heart of secularism was seen an inadmissible divorcing of God and public affairs.

That some are beginning to think more benignly of secularism is a direct outgrowth of the renewal of Christian theology. Many "forgotten" facets of the Christian mysteries have been restored to prominence. One of these is that God is in the world as well as in his Church, and that he uses not only the Church but even the world to form his people for himself.

For some writers this renewed awareness has become an excuse for displaying their secret atheism. Enamored of the world and of man's role in it, they cry: "God is dead" — and they mean it. For them Christ means nothing but the spirit of unrestrained humanism, and the first duty of men is to free themselves of the "shackles" of all organized, and especially revealed, religion.

Other writers, like the Protestant theologians Altizer and Hamilton, have been led by this new world-awareness to attempt some real theologizing. Seemingly they seek a clarification of God's presence and influence regarding man in Christ, both during Christ's life on earth and after his resurrection. Whether their "God is dead" notions imply a high-level agnosticism or an exaggerated concept of his presence in the world, to the point of losing his own real identity as an infinite Being apart from the world, is difficult to say.

With other writers this renewed awareness leads to something still different. The language they use is often akin to that of real atheists, and for this reason they are easily misunderstood. These men are "Christian atheists," however — Protestant writers like J. A. T. Robinson and Harvey Cox — and deserve a serious hearing.

Their thought seems to be that Christian ideas and terminology, organizations and procedures, even Christian values, have in great part lost a creative hold on the imagination of modern man. Christianity, they say, has lost its spirit, and has settled for acceptance as an institution. It has become a "system," an "establishment," a structured organization of "middle-class" conventions and attitudes. At best it has become a comedy of the gospel.

What these "Christian atheists" seem to be calling for is nothing short of an internal revolution within Christianity. Their aim is to expose, even explode, many of the pet ideas and reaction-patterns of the Churches. Specifically, they level their barrages at the Churches' typical concern for God at the expense of men. The world, they say, is the proper sphere of the Churches, not the sanctuary; loving and serving men in the world is their business, not collecting dues, enforcing rules, and filling pews.

A Catholic Response

To this line of thought a Catholic can react very sympathetically. Following Vatican II, in fact, he must. He will be prompted, however, to approach the matter of reducing *ecclesiasticism* along a somewhat different line. Because of his particular understanding of what Christianity is, he will set certain limits to the scope of this kind of thinking; his search for relevancy will be especially tempered by fidelity to the dogmas of his Church.

What a Catholic might suggest is that the new awareness of man and the world should awaken an *additional* rather than an *alternate* perspective toward the Church. God is not so much dead today as man is alive; Christianity is not so much decadent as the world is in need.

A Catholic can agree that for too long now the Church has been the possessor of an inadequate understanding of man and the world. God and his saving interventions have too long held an unbalanced priority. That the primacy of God and the main sources of his grace prompt the Church to assign a certain priority to worship and ecclesiastical loyalty is one thing. That this should lead to a regrettable passivity, to an exaggerated confidence in God's providence, to an isolationist view of Christian life in the world is quite another. The *Constitution on the Church in the Modern World* is a humble acknowledgment on the part of the Catholic Church that the latter has long been the actual situation.

Assigning man as the "immediate" object of the Church's total endeavor and restructuring the whole program of "ecclesiasticism" in that light are not at all opposed to the supremacy of God. It is, rather, an asserting of that supremacy through a "discovery" and implementation of his plan.

Revelation gives no indication that grace has replaced human nature, or that life in the Church is a substitute for life in the world. Neither is Christ the sole source of the knowledge and energy upon which man's salvation and happiness hinge.

True, Christ alone gives grace; but grace is neither imagination, intelligence, nor initiative. True, Christ alone gives the gospel; but the gospel is not a manual of techniques.

Man's well-being in the world is a thing for man to achieve, not God. Peace and justice, opportunity and accomplishment are man's responsibility, not God's. Man can "make or break" his individual and communal life in the world, and God has in no way committed himself to intervene. In Christian faith he bestows a vision of what can and should be, and in the sacred ministrations of his Church he bestows remedies unto that vision's accomplishment. His Church and its participants can well be at fault in misconceiving and misapplying these gifts. It must reap the fruit of its own ignorance, however, and the world along with it will suffer as a consequence.

Readings

Abbott & Gallagher (eds.), *Pastoral Constitution on the Church in the Modern World*, in *The Documents of Vatican II* (New York: Guild Press, 1966).

Adolphs, Robert, *Grave of God* (New York: Harper & Row, 1966).

Bent, Charles, S.J., *The Death-of-God Movement* (New York: Paulist Press, 1967).

"Commonweal Papers # 1: God," *Commonweal*, February 10, 1967.

Cox, Harvey, *On Not Leaving It to the Snake* (New York: Macmillan, 1967).

Miller, John H., C.S.C. (ed.), *Vatican II: An Interfaith Appraisal* (South Bend, Ind.: University of Notre Dame Press, 1966), especially "The Constitution on the Church in the Modern World," by Most Reverend Mark G. McGrath, C.S.C., p. 397 ff.; and "The Church in the World Today — Challenge to Theology," by Very Reverend Joseph Gremillion, p. 521 ff.

Proceedings of the 21st Annual Convention of the Catholic Theological Society of America, Vol. 21, 1967, "What Is Christian Secularity?" by Thomas E. Clarke, S.J., p. 201 ff.; and "American Unbelief and the Death of God," by Anthony T. Padovano, p. 113 ff.

Spirituality in the Secular City, Concilium No. 19 (New York: Paulist Press, 1967).

Trevor, Meriol, *Pope John* (Garden City, N. Y.: Doubleday, 1967).

PROCESS

Alterations

As features of the present day, personalism and secularism do not stand in isolation. They are closely related to each other and share common roots in something else. What they spring from is actually of greater influence, being more pervasive and formative of the modern mood. For lack of a better term this root factor can be named *process*, and it stands for modern man's realization that both his world and his thoughts about his world only gradually arrive at fullness. Before describing this realization more fully, however, a glance at some of the things that have inspired it seems in order.

Perhaps the most revolutionary alteration of man's understanding of the world has occurred over the past century in the physical sciences. Biology is a case in point. With increasing conviction this science is playing host to the theory of evolution.

Change has always been known in nonliving things, and in a sense has always been the very sign of life in living things. What has only become clearly recognized in the past hundred years, however, is that both nonliving and living things have developed out of things more primitive in design and ability than themselves. What is more, they are themselves on the way to becoming newer and higher things.

Since evolution has occurred in the past, scientists tell us, everything supports the conclusion that it continues in the present, and will do so in the future. Though dreadfully slow, even undetectable in its progress, evolution goes on, nonetheless. Millions of years ago the present world of things was inconceivable; by the same token, the world of the future is at present unimaginable. Day by day patterns of biological alteration continue, and the physical world of the future silently takes form.

Philosophy also contends with what seems to be a major alteration, this one concerning human nature. Generally speaking, until the present day man's nature has been understood primarily in the light of early Greek reflections. Man was thought to be fully formed as to his essential make-up, and the subject of fundamentally unchanging purposes and experiences. Today, on the other hand, philosophers are tending to conclude that this traditional understanding of man simply does not square with the facts. There is a richness to human nature, they say, that only gradually works itself to the surface of man's consciousness. With each successive awakening, moreover, it falls to man to reshape both his thinking and his attitudes toward himself, his achievements and his possibilities.

Consider, for example, woman in society. Seven hundred years ago, it would have been a rare person who claimed for her an indispensable role in public life. Today one would not be orthodox who denied it. Something has happened during the intervening centuries to awaken in woman a level of humanness not previously suspected. The impact of this awakening has been inescapably to make her the social partner of man in molding public life.

Another alteration concerns humanity's experience of the marital relationship. What was formerly taken as a mere functional union has in the past century become a relationship in which personal values are assuming quite authentic primacy over those of a functional kind. What has happened? Again, philosophers see a "surfacing" of a level of humanness previously unsuspected, a level to be explained mainly in terms of modern psychology and personalism, to say nothing of the meaning and role of sex.

War and international relations are the subjects of yet another alteration in man's experience. If historians are to be believed, war, for example, was at one time a casual, even reputable project. Scripture itself refers casually to "the season when kings go to war." Today a swelling wave of feeling makes the very idea of war intolerable. In the same vein unrestrained nationalism, once a matter of honor, is today considered a glaring disregard of human values. And pertaining to the same picture are such things as torture, capital punishment, colonialism, and underdeveloped peoples — all of which are subjects today of condemnation or alleviation, as the case may be. Here, again, is a "surfacing" of richer depths of humanness, a change in man, according to many philosophers.

Mere Change or Real Growth?

To all these alterations — and there are many others — one can bring different attitudes. Since they are mere trends, often entwined with exaggerations and contradictions, they can be seen as fundamentally false and dangerous. As often as not they pose a real threat to what has laboriously been developed and organized over the years. Because antiwar and civil rights demonstrations, for example, can be disorderly and destructive they are roundly condemned by some. Because recasting marriage along personalistic lines or acknowledging the likelihood of biological evolution runs counter to long established and neatly drawn lines of thought and practice, advocates of adjustment also incur the censure of some.

Another attitude is to interpret these alterations as real changes in man's recognition of what traditional theories and systems have always implied or basically allowed for. They can be called new emphases on what man has always known and sought, but they do not reflect any real modification either of man or the world, at least not in any sense that matters.

A third attitude sees in these alterations not mere change, but growth, development, and even evolution in the world, man, and human affairs. This is the attitude that can be given the name *process*, namely, the realization that the world of man, including man himself, and man's knowledge of his world only gradually come to fullness. The idea is that of all things being in becoming, the idea of continuing creation, the idea of time and history as ingredients of everything in the world. Widely felt and, like everything else of significance, having its roots in the past, this attitude has two major representatives today: Pierre Teilhard de Chardin and Marshall McLuhan.

De Chardin

Regarding Teilhard de Chardin, it is difficult to be either indifferent or open-minded. The reason for this is, on the one hand, that his theorizing cuts such a mortal swath across the stock of traditional thinking, and, on the other hand, that he has been the subject of not a little prejudiced criticism.

By his own admission, De Chardin was a "visionary" rather than a technical analyst. He was concerned with drawing together the threads of awareness typical of modern man, and forging these into a "possible" or "suggested" unity. The unity he presents is original and unique; what he puts into it, however, was drawn from scholars in science, philosophy, and theology, little or none of it being at all new.

He intended his vision as a possible bridge between "secularistic" scientists and the Church. In no sense was he grinding an axe against the ecclesiastical *status quo*; his most productive years came long before the prevailing distinction between liberals and conservatives in the Church.

Neither did De Chardin intend his writings to be a last word on anything. His express purpose was to present only a beginning, an opening of conversation. He knew well the incapacity of his own mind to carry the full expanse of the unity he saw in contemporary discoveries and experiences. He intended only to draw its general lines, and he pleaded that if others thought him correct they themselves would struggle with filling in the details.

From a theological point of view, the trouble with De Chardin's "vision" is that it seems to leave little or no room for such traditional doctrines as the distinction between nature and supernature, the special creation of man, sin, redemption, and freedom. What must be recalled, though, is that he framed his thought in the midst of the early twentieth-century European theological renewal, and time and again he put his ideas to the test with leading thinkers of the day. Moreover, that his "vision" calls for a recasting of some points of theology is not of itself a liability. If one takes time to look, in fact, most of the necessary recasting of the theological points in question has already been done, quite independently of defending or condemning De Chardin.

Another problem concerns the scientists to whom he was primarily addressing himself. His words are laden with implications for faith, religion and morality. His appeal is that scientists see in their combined achievements a base for opening themselves to the *Something Beyond* to which these achievements point. For many scientists this appeal is simply too much; not only do they dismiss it, they belittle the "fabrication" at its base. For many others, however, there is no doubt that De Chardin raised a challenge not easily forgotten. For these, at least, few have done as much as he in this most difficult area of dialogue.

In summary the "vision" of De Chardin is evolutionary process applied to the total creative and saving plan of God. Convinced of the evolution of the physical universe and of man, De Chardin went on to see evolution continuing consciously and freely in the life of man. Charged with energies both of humanness and grace, man is in process of gradual liberation from individualism through personalism to community. By choice man can advance or retard this process. Profoundly optimistic, both for humanistic and Christian reasons, De Chardin was convinced, however, that this process will continually advance, ultimately achieving Point Omega wherein a universal community of men bonded in the Spirit of Christ and the purest personalism will come permanently to be.

The origin of this process is the immensely creative love of God, and at every stage of the way this same love is a power of continuing creation. Christ, grace, and the Church are superabundant outpourings of this love, geared specifically to rounding out and bringing the total process to completion. At the other end of this process is again the love of God, considered now as a measureless power of attraction, drawing the process toward the same end. Point Omega is this very love, preluded in Christ and the Church, now wholly shared by those who faithfully contributed to its achievement.

Typical of De Chardin's "vision" is the mysterious grandeur of matter. As he saw it, matter is the great "sacrament" of God and of Christ in creation. It is the bearer of the creative love that originates, directs, and draws the world process onward. If he had done nothing else, De Chardin has left a legacy of the sacredness of things material which should win him the undying appreciation of modern, technological, matter-immersed man.

Marshall McLuhan

Of quite a different cast is Marshall McLuhan, contemporary social philosopher. *Process* for this thinker is the impact of communications media on man. As a society communicates, he stresses, so it will become.

As McLuhan sees the human scene, man's thinking and feeling about the world and himself, even the world that he builds, is the unseen product of the way he addresses himself at any time in his history. From the beginning to the present time man is both victim and product of his communications. Primitive man, for example, was in communion with nature, was bonded in tribal loyalty, was spontaneously responsive to his surroundings because his media of communication were face-to-face encounter, conversation, and symbols of a material kind. With the invention of printing, on the other hand, man changed to a more analytic, calculated, and mental mode of living. Capable then of representing his experiences and feelings in printed symbols, man became less personal, more tightly organized, ambitious to control his surroundings, intellectual rather than spontaneous.

Today, especially under the influence of television, something different is happening again. The impact of movies was to deaden or at least decrease the wholeness of responsiveness even more than printing. With television, however, and to a less extent with radio, responsiveness is again heightened. There is something about television, McLuhan asserts, that makes for personal participation; it is a "cool" medium of communication in that it leaves details to be filled in by the imagination of the viewer. Television draws the viewer actively into the situation; it also places the situation directly in the presence of the viewer. And what is true of television, according to McLuhan, is equally true of organizational structures that are geared to maximum involvement; loosely programed projects are far more inducive to spontaneous participation, are far more "cool," than those tightly drawn and legislated.

What McLuhan is driving at can be seen only by enlarging the television experience to the same universal proportions as the effect of printing. The impact of the television medium, he says, will be staggering, and only its beginning can now be seen. Its influence will be to make man conscious again of his fellowman and real world — in the flesh, in feelings, in suffering and happiness, in struggles. It is the tribal experience all over again, only now on a universal level: man is being made a spontaneous participant in the world community.

With George Leonard in *Look* magazine, July 25, 1967, McLuhan has speculated that one sign of this transition is already evident in the relationship between the sexes. The typical roles of he-man and coy female no longer match the personal experiences of man and woman. Time will see man and woman, these authors predict, more and more forging their relationships simply in terms of their effort to be persons; passing away is the day of persons meeting one another simply as sex symbols.

Readings

Culkin, John H., S.J., "A Schoolman's Guide to Marshall McLuhan," *Saturday Review*, March 18, 1967.

De Lubac, Henri, S.J., *The Religion of Teilhard de Chardin* (New York: Desclee, 1967).

Faricy, Robert, S.J., *Theilhard de Chardin's Theology of the Christian in the World* (New York: Sheed & Ward, 1967).

Francoeur, Robert T., *Perspective in Evolution* (Baltimore: Helicon, 1965).

McLuhan, Marshall, *Understanding Media* (New York: New American Library, 1964).

Nogar, Raymond J., O.P., *The Wisdom of Evolution* (New York: Doubleday & Co., 1963).

O'Meara, Thomas F., O.P., "Liturgy Hot and Cool," *Worship*, April, 1968, pp. 215–222.

SERVICE

Signs of the Times

Among the characteristic features of the mid-twentieth century surely the strangest has been the "Hippie" movement. Though there were counterparts in preceding generations, the Hippies exhibit several impressive differences. In sheer numbers, for example, they have been extraordinary; *Time* magazine reported a colony of 10,000 in San Francisco during the Summer of 1967, and Hippies themselves estimated there were some 300,000 across the country that same year.

Another difference, perhaps the most remarkable, has been the intellectual and socio-economic status of the movement's reputed leaders and mainstream representatives. According to conventional standards, countless Hippies could have claimed rightful rank among the most promising persons in the nation.

Hippiedom has been a protest movement, but not of a conventional kind. Whereas most protests aim at securing values treasured by conventional society, the Hippies represent a peaceful and often silent statement to the effect that conventional society with all its values "can simply go hang." It is a quaint but telling accusation against the "Establishment" that in countless ways its structures — government, schools, homes, churches, professions — have written out of their program the very thing for which they are supposed to exist: to let people develop, to let them be themselves, to let them be together and do together what they want.

The sweeping freedoms claimed by the Hippies are themselves enough to make many deeply distrustful of the movement. Their dirtiness, lack of sexual restraint, and above all their widespread use of drugs have only served to confirm this distrust.

Yet, there has also been a fascination and fondness for the "flower children" widely felt. Their dressing style, outlandish as it is, has not been found wholly distasteful. The sight of a number of them completely neutralizing the seriousness of National Guardsmen by poking daisies into their brandished gun barrels was truly captivating.

Above all, though, it is their protestations of love and peaceableness toward everyone that has won them countless sympathizers. And some of the Hippies actually practice what they preach: the volunteer groups who operate farms and stores, and who share their "pads," so that their colony compatriots might have food, clothing, and shelter, are an eloquent witness to their genuineness.

Their witness is above all what makes at least some of the Hippies real "prophets" of the times deserving of respect. It is also what links Hippiedom with other movements of the day, more conventional in kind, which go together to indicate a very real mood and trend. For lack of a better word this impulse can be called a spirit of *service*.

The success of the Peace Corps, enhanced as it is by the preference shown it by the late President Kennedy, is perhaps the most graphic witness to this spirit. Participation in the Papal Volunteers and in home and foreign lay missionary projects is a similar witness within the Church. On a less organized level the wide response to civil rights and peace demonstrations is part of the same picture. People today, especially the young, want to be involved in the creating of a world more truly reflective of man's dignity.

Obviously anyone with even a little knowledge of history, to say nothing of adolescent psychology, will know that the present generation is not unique in this will to serve. The Romantics of the past century are a case in point; and where is the teacher who has never heard young people declare their love of people and their ambition to pursue a career that entails working with them?

Today's impulse toward service is different, nonetheless; and any number of factors illustrate this. There is, for example, a well-founded awareness in our time that unless men begin to have a more genuine mutual regard they can easily destroy themselves.

There is also a greater awareness of man's personal nature, of the uniqueness and dignity of each individual, of each person's right to respect and acceptance.

Culturally, due mainly to improved means of communication and travel, there is also an increased sensitivity to the irreplaceable richness of different racial and social groups. Economically, the very industrial character of modern society is steadily shifting toward a predominance of the service industries, much as our society once shifted from agriculture to manufacturing.

In light of all this one cannot be merely casual or patronizing about the service-impetus so apparent in so many young people today. There is more here than ordinary youthful idealism. Those who are service-centered today not only have a richer intuition of humanity's possibilities and needs — their opportunities for knowing these are greater — but an equally perceptive grasp of basic techniques for dealing with them. The urge of young people today toward group discussions and group planning, toward dialogue and participation with others, is fundamentally part of this basic instinct.

"The times, they are a changin'," sings Bob Dylon. If Vatican II can see the contemporary emergence of socialization as a product of God's creative and saving purposes, one should be prepared to do no less in the case of the will to serve animating so many modern young people. Surely contemporary theology presents an inspiring basis for this preparedness.

Charisms

One of the richest rediscoveries of modern theology is the charismatic nature of the Church. This point, once so prominent in the awareness of Christians but neglected in recent centuries by way of reaction to regrettable excesses, has regained a rightful primacy. Vatican II's *Constitution on the Church* ratifies it, the American bishops' *Pastoral on the Church in Our Day* clarifies it, and writers are at pains today to explain and broadcast it — to the advantage of all.

Simply stated, the charismatic nature of the Church means that the people of God, hierarchy and laity alike, possess the fullness of Christ's Spirit for the fulfilling of the saving mission laid upon them. This Spirit touches all of God's people, but in different ways. To each is given a dowry of power for doing his or her share in the total project of the Church:

> . . . It should be clear by now that the charismata are not limited to a small group of persons, but are granted to Christians communally and individually. Every Christian has his charisma. . . . Whoever has received the Spirit, shares in the gifts of the Spirit. The charisma is therefore not the privilege of a few elect, based on religious "enthusiasm" or on office, but of the whole Church as the community of all the faithful (Hans Küng).

Charisms, in a word, are service-graces, whether completely new abilities given with sanctifying grace, or refinements of natural abilities for the sake of impelling one's natural individuality toward participation in Christ's mission. They are gifts bestowed not so much for the sake of one's own growth in Christ as for the sake of the growth of others.

Some charisms are wholly exceptional, like the power to work miracles. Others are more official, taking expression through certain offices in the Church, like teaching and legislating authority, infallibility, and the ministerial power of priesthood. For the rest, charisms are capabilities for turning ordinary things into telling moments of contribution to the cause of Christ. They may be rooted in one's mind, for the sake of understanding and speaking; in one's will, for the sake of decision-making and constancy; in one's feelings, for the sake of gentleness and sympathy; or in one's body, for the sake of work, endurance, or even just appearance. Any aspect of a person's being can be touched by a charismatic gift, and every aspect of the Church's life stands in need of charismatic support and expression.

Chief among the charisms, according to St. Paul at least, and one that inevitably is offered all the faithful, is the charism of charity. Love is the greatest service which the Church is endowed to give, and for its dispensing everyone in the Church is prepared by the service-grace called charity. Developing and manifesting this gift is the fundamental vocation of all Christians.

Vocation

Neither charity nor any other Christian charism takes expression in a vacuum, however. There is, of course, a certain general use to be made of them as need or authentic impulse dictates, always in keeping with the real work and style of Christ's Spirit. But their ordinary sphere of proper expression is one's state of life. This, in turn, means that charisms are ordinarily associated with a further charism, that of personal vocation. Here, especially, contemporary theology has an important word for the prevailing mood of service.

Happily the day has passed when vocation meant only priestly and religious callings. Today, in keeping with its older and richer meaning, vocation is rightly applied to any and every way of life in agreement with God's creative and saving purposes.

What this implies is that God works his purposes toward men by means of the vocations he bestows. Vocations are, thus, so many different ways of sharing in God's wisdom, power, and love toward men.

Analyzed more closely, a vocation is a *gift*, a *conditioning* for a special task, and a *summons* to service. Especially to be noted is the harmony between a vocation and the one possessing it. A vocation is not a thing foreign to a person; neither is it something external. Rooted in a person's being, a vocation arises from within. It is one's entire being shaped for a role in God's plan.

Seldom is this element of harmony so strict, however, as to oblige compliance. Father Bernard Häring, a contemporary moralist, would tend to disagree. Urging that God's will is precisely his gifts to men, Father Häring is of the opinion that to disregard a clearly perceived vocation is to sin.

Approaching the matter of vocation from the perspective of sin, however, is to cloud the issue; and Father Häring would agree. Certainty regarding a vocation is surely quite rare, and when it is present an individual will know his obligation.

Central to vocation is opportunity, not obligation. Vocation denotes suitability: the element of harmony makes one way of life preferable, more advantageous, both to oneself and to God's purposes. A vocation is a line of direction in one's being fully agreeable to personal make-up and to God's plan. Better yet, it is an inborn sense of direction, thus agreeable.

By choosing an alternate one takes a line of direction not as instinctive or connatural to oneself and God's designs. In aim and possibility this alternate may be as true and predictable as one's vocation. In pratice, however, it may well be less direct and adapted: it may well feature more difficulty than satisfaction, more output than return, more acts than meaning.

All vocations — and everybody has one — are meant to serve the mission of Christ. All vocations are thus Christian in character, though not in the same way.

Some vocations have a *general* Christian character. These flow directly from a person's natural make-up and follow closely the lines of human nature. Their Christian character consists in their capacity to be exercised in the name of Christ and for the sake of his purposes. They *become* Christian, in other words, under the influence of charismatic grace and Christian motivation.

Other vocations have a *specific* Christian character. These flow directly from grace, and depart notably, at times radically, from the lines of human nature. The priesthood and religious life are but two examples of these. Being obviously Christian, these vocations are less obviously *human.* In theory, according to Pius XII, the humanness of these vocations is assured by the influence of compensating graces. In practice it is a matter of their possessors' personality and life-style.

Service-Centered Christians

At the present time vocations dealing with the temporal and social well-being of men are being preferred by service-centered Christians to vocations to the priesthood and religious life. One might wonder whether this implies a lessening of the latter vocations or simply an increase of alternate choices. In either event, God may well be trying to tell his people something.

On the one hand, the service of men in their temporal and social needs is of such glaring importance today that Christians dare not miss the call of the hour. On the other hand, both priesthood and religious life have become so identified with "institutionalism" as to have lost not only their own identity as dynamic and creative service roles but their very image of being service-centered at all.

Surely one can argue the matter, and adults might enjoy the discussion. But service-centered youth today could hardly care less. They want to be where the action is, and right now the action is in the area of the social apostolate. This is the bare fact of the matter, and it should not be missed.

With an eye to charisms and vocations it remains only to guide the service enthusiasms of youthful Christians in a direction most harmonious with themselves and the needs of the times. Properly guided, rather than debunked or belittled, these enthusiasms may well be the stuff from which the total Christian apostolate of tomorrow will be molded.

Readings

Abbott & Gallagher (eds.), *Dogmatic Constitution on the Church,* Chap. 2, in *The Documents of Vatican II* (New York: Guild Press, 1966).

The Church in Our Day, Pastoral Letter of the American Catholic Bishops (Washington, D. C.: U. S. Catholic Conference, 1968).

Häring, Bernard, C.Ss.R., *The Law of Christ* (Westminster, Md.: Newman, 1961), Vol. 1, Chap. 6.

"The Hippies: Philosophy of a Subculture," *Time* magazine, July 7, 1967.

Küng, Hans, "The Charismatic Structure of the Church," Concilium No. 4 (New York: Paulist Press, 1965), *The Church and Ecumenism.*

Rahner, Karl, S.J., *The Dynamic Element in the Church* (New York: Herder, 1964).

Van Kaam, Adrian, *Personality Fulfillment in the Spiritual Life* (Wilkes-Barre, Pa.: Dimension Books, 1966).

——— *Personality Fulfillment in the Religious Life* (Wilkes-Barre, Pa.: Dimension Books, 1967).

PART TWO

Fundamental Notions

REVELATION

Past and Present Notions

In recent centuries theologians have tended to explain revelation as God's communicating special knowledge to man. The content of revelation has been regarded as a deposit of special truths: of new insights into God's life and love, new certainties regarding creatures, new awarenesses of gifts among men. Correspondingly, the process of revelation has been described as divine speech — God telling men the secrets of his being and purposes. The special truths in question have been seen as wholly contained in the teachings of the Church, some as dogmas and others as unformulated convictions carried in the data of Scripture and Tradition. God's statement of these truths, on the other hand, has been seen as completed since the death of the apostles.

Contemporary theologians find this picture quite inadequate, insisting that it puts what is secondary where what is primary belongs. They are convinced that the Bible and even the traditional theology present a far different portrait.

The sketch of revelation they draw has God in the center, not man's understanding. Revelation, they say, is God himself in the very act of disclosing himself as Savior. Revelation is incident or happening; understanding is but aspect or aftermath.

The content of revelation, then, is God himself in saving activity; its process is his special presence and management within human history. In a word, God makes himself present and active in human history in a saving way, and gives man to understand this — this is revelation according to contemporary theologians.

In light of this, dogmas and unformulated convictions of the Church take on a different hue. They stand now more in relation to revelation than as being its exclusive embodiment. Revelation, moreover, is seen as continuing, in both content and process.

Points of Contemporary Emphasis

These differences between past and present theologians must not be exaggerated. While emphasizing truths, past theologians always insisted that these dealt with God himself and his saving love. Similarly, though Vatican II endorsed the view of contemporary theologians, Vatican I, a century ago, bore witness that past theologians always held that ultimately the content of revelation is God himself.

Neither are past and present theologians wholly in disagreement regarding the process of revelation. Contemporary theologians are quick to acknowledge that direct divine "speech" is the preferred means of revelation in the Bible, as is clearly shown in the discourses of the prophets and of Jesus.

Intimate to the contemporary view, nonetheless, is the realization that these points of agreement do not tell the whole story. There are significant points of difference begging for emphasis.

One of these is the broader meaning given God's "word," a meaning beyond that of mere knowledge communication. The Bible sees God's "word" primarily as God's activity: he "speaks" both when creating and saving. Even when using "word" as direct knowledge communication, the Bible uses it first for God's presence and intervention, and only then for the "message" embodied in that intervention.

> It goes without saying that no biblical theologian would deny that the divine word plays a decisive role in the whole of revelation. However, it also becomes immediately evident that hardly any single event of revelation can be formulated exclusively in the category of conceptual speech. Though "God's word" is used as the customary designation of the revelatory event, "word" is understood as the Hebrew *dābār* — often in direct antithesis to the intellectual "Greek" understanding — in a much fuller sense than merely as a means of communication. The word of God in the biblical sense is first and foremost an expression of the divine will: it is filled with might and power, it is immediately creative, it is what lies behind all that occurs, especially salvation history. In the deepest sense, the "word" of God is definitively the eternal Word become man in Christ (Bulst).

Another difference is revelation's historical character. Rather than a spectacular "intrusion" into human affairs — as might be

God's announcing "special truths" — revelation takes real form only in the concrete data of human history: in people, places, times, incidents. It is an "awakening" to the Reality "managing" this data.

> This conception of revelation *in* history has two effects. First of all, it *gives value* to history. If God intervenes in history and manifests His will, historical events themselves acquire a new dimension: they become the bearers of God's intentions and give history a meaning, a sense of direction. . . . The idea of revelation *in* history thus gives revelation an intense character of *actualization*. God is He who, at every instant, can intervene and change the course of events: He is near, He is there, unforeseeable in His interventions as well as in His effects. Always, man must look to His coming (Latourelle).

Accommodated to man as he stands amid the data of his history, revelation is a process whose tempo, extension, and depth is decided for the most part by man's own perceptive capacities and his actual responses at any given moment of his individual and/or collective history.

> God began the dialogue at the level at which man was to be found. . . . Every act of love on God's part, every response on man's part, changed the revelatory position of man. . . . The most amazing thing about revelation, it would seem, is that the sins of men not only did not break off the relation, but in a certain sense became part of the revelational process. . . . God knew that he must gently draw man forward, not simply by disregarding his failures, but by using even failure to bring man to see what man is and what God is (Moran).

In this process God, of course, always keeps the upper hand. One aspect of revelation, therefore, is God's making men sensitive to the "salvation potential" coursing through their historical experiences. Another is that he planned both this sensitivity and salvation potential to reach fullness in the personal history of Jesus.

Revelation Continues

What mainly distinguishes the contemporary view is its conception of revelation's continuance. This in turn rests on a particular conception of Christ's role in revelation's history.

Past theologians tended to see Christ as the final installment of God's saving communications. Contemporary theologians tend to see him as in some way the termination of "salvation history," the culmination of God's impregnating history with salvation potential.

The gist of both views is that the historical facts of Christ's life are in some way "transplanted" into all subsequent history. The continuance of revelation is thus commonly seen as a doctrinal or sacramental handing on of the "continuing past" of Christ. However:

> . . . either revelation is constituted by events in the experience of men in the past and is no longer with us because their experience has ceased; or revelation consists of truths not irrevocably tied to temporal events but communicable through propositions from one generation to another. . . . When the protest against a revelation of "mere truths" has been heard the question remains: How can revelation be anything other than truths or objects if it is handed down from one generation to another; or, reversing the question, how can a revelation consisting of personal events in the past ever be a present revelation? (Moran)

Organic to both views, then, is the need of clarification. Since the contemporary view sponsors the conclusion that "there is no revelation unless God is now acting and unless a human consciousness is now responding," it too must in some clearer way get revelation out of the past and into the present.

> The key to a personal revelation in the twentieth century lies in the emergence of a human consciousness that is entirely receptive to God revealing and that remains among men to continue that revelation. It is to that person that we now turn (Moran).

Strategic, in other words, is a more adequate understanding of Christ as not only the embodiment of all revelation but as its continuing agent.

Contemporary theologians agree that revelation continues through Christ. What they do not always make clear is that it is the present revelation of Christ that continues.

Thus it is to be well noted that the continuance of revelation consists in Christ's bringing the people of God to an ever deeper experiencing of his own personal revelation, that which is his own by reason of his enthronement at the "right hand of the Father."

Revelation continues and grows as a movement of deepening and expanding realization of what Christ now experiences in glory. He shares with men, gradually — through doctrines, sacraments, and historical "arrangements" — what he won in himself in their name.

Focused and Diffused Revelation

Intimate to the preceding is the fact that while on earth Christ revealed the Father in a human way. Because of his earth-bound humanity his sayings and doings always fell short of being adequate expressions of what he himself was ever more fully experiencing.

Similarly, the apostles spoke of "that which they had looked upon and touched," always, however, with the radical inability to express exactly what they had encountered.

The statement of revelation given the Church by Christ and the apostles, therefore, is essentially a human and limited description of the Reality with which it deals; and the same is true of the Church's dogmas and unformulated convictions.

This statement, nonetheless, is *focused* revelation; Christ has arranged that it be an unerring channel of ever clearer perception.

> He does not leave His doctrine to the chance of history and individual interpretation. He protects it first of all by handing it down through a charism of *inspiration*, then He entrusts it to a Church which He fortifies with a charism of *infallibility* to preserve, defend, propose, and authentically interpret revelation. The Church, which is the Bride of Christ, possesses His word as a deposit which she meditates and assimilates unceasingly in the light of the Spirit. Without this divinely established magisterium, and without the special assistance of the Spirit, we gladly concede that it is impossible to conceive of a doctrine, even though divine in origin, which could escape the fluctuations of history (Latourelle).

Quite otherwise is the *diffused* revelation that impregnates nature and history in non-Christian form. Though also the "word" of Christ, powerful unto insights and salvation, this revelation is even less adequate to the saving Reality than the focused descriptions given by Christ, the apostles, and the Church.

For the vast majority of men, past and present, however, this is the only operative form of revelation; it awakens the multitudes whom Karl Rahner has styled "anonymous Christians." In a particular setting, moreover, it may well be more pregnant with "saving awareness" than its focused counterpart — witness, for example, Hinduism:

> The spiritual history of Hinduism is full of instances parallel to that of Christ finding in the non-Jewish woman or the Roman officer more faith than in the House of Israel. That is to say, the spiritual history of Hinduism in the past as well as in the present tells us of true virtue, of real sanctity, of authentic mysticism, and I would even dare to say, of undeniable miracles and true charity. . . . An ontological study of history from a theological point of view proves that Divine Providence has been looking after all his children, and that there is a Christian economy in history in which Hinduism cannot be fully rejected, but in which it finds its providential place. What other means of salvation has God — Christ — provided for the people of India down the ages, even before the appearance of historical Christianity? . . . The ultimate core of salvation does indeed lie in the unutterable depths of the human person, but the normal divine preparation for this ultimate step goes through the more tangible channels of the established religion, even if they cannot provide the perfect means of salvation (Panikkar).

Diffused and focused revelation, for all that, are not essentially separable. Though separated in structure, their lines of disclosure and development are identical. They move, moreover, toward convergence — whether in time or eternity.

Readings

Bulst, Werner, *Revelation* (New York: Herder & Herder, 1965).

Latourelle, Rene, S.J., *The Theology of Revelation* (New York: Alba House, 1966).

Moran, Gabriel, F.S.C., *The Theology of Revelation* (New York: Herder & Herder, 1966).

Panikkar, Raymond, "Hinduism and Christianity," *Cross Currents,* Winter, 1963.

FAITH

The Object of Christian Faith

First to be noted about Christian faith is its *object*. Though seeming to be a multitude of "things" — dogmas, institutions, practices — the object of Christian faith is in final analysis a Person. Essentially, Christian faith is an accepting of Jesus Christ as Son and Messiah of God.

Things of faith have, it is true, a definite bearing on the object of Christian faith. They are aspects and manifestations of that object. Christian dogmas, for example, are conceptual aspects — ideas set down in words — of the mystery of Christ. Institutions like the sacraments and the Church, on the other hand, are manifestations of Christ as he continues to be present and active in the world.

Things of faith thus embody — but only to a degree — the content or presence of the object of Christian faith. They are not objects of Christian faith independently of that which they represent or convey. Neither are they believed so much for what they are in themselves as for what they are in symbol. They are believed because the Person they describe or manifest is believed. Faith in Christ provides the "ground" for faith in the things of faith. Belief in Christ stands behind, underlies, supports, makes sense of belief in them.

One cannot, for all that, be casual about faith in the things of faith, as though belief in Christ independently of all other considerations alone really mattered. Authentic Christian faith accepts Christ in his fullness, not only in his Person but in his meaning and forms of continuance as well. Thus, the object of Christian faith has a specific totality: it is Christ, to be sure, but Christ as he is in himself, as he is known in Christian dogmas, and as he is present and active in Christian institutions and practices.

Clarifying the relationship between faith in Christ and faith in the things of faith is one of the key contributions of contemporary theology.

In recent centuries the object of Christian faith has been explained primarily in terms of things. As often as not Christ himself has been presented as but one in a series of things to be held on faith. Revelation — as was shown in the preceding chapter — has been conceived as the collectivity of these things.

The product of many causes, this thing-emphasis has been for the most part unfortunate. Faith has become more a doctrinal, even sectarian, position than a knowing of Christ. Concentrating unduly on the things of Christ, Christians have become ignorant of Christ himself. Even the things of Christ have themselves been misconceived, disassociated as they have been from him who is their verification and content.

Contemporary theologians attempt to repair this state of affairs by restating the older and more authentic understanding of Christian faith. According to that understanding Christ alone is the primary and all-pervading object of Christian faith. Not even God, so to speak, has primacy here. What Christians believe in first, last, and always is Jesus the Lord. It is belief in him that initiates and substantiates Christian belief in God and the things of God.

The Act of Christian Faith

Theologians today also have much to say about the act of Christian faith. Here too they correct an imbalance of recent centuries.

In line with their reflections on the object of Christian faith they see the act of Christian faith as a free and personal attachment to Christ, a state of heart — not just of mind — toward Christ and the things that describe and disclose him. The key idea here is that of personal relationship and commitment — personal espousal.

As an act, Christian faith is no mere mental assent to the truth of things divinely revealed and set forth by the Church. It is that, to be sure — the point emphasized in recent centuries — but also much more. Though one might say that in body the act of Christian faith is an intellectual recognition of the truth of Christ and the things of Christ, in soul it is a sacrificial willingness "to step into the future wholly under his auspices." In final analysis, then, the act of Christian faith is far more a matter of will than of mind.

Traditional theology has always acknowledged this insofar as the act of Christian faith is a decision — a choice — made in the face of indications rather than evidence. Nothing, after all, compels Christian belief, neither external arguments nor internal experiences. Inevitably a credibility gap exists between what leads to faith and an act of faith, which is as true of faith in Christ as faith in any other person or thing. Only a free decision bridges this gap.

What has not always been stressed — the point emphasized by modern theology — is that the act of Christian faith is a decision regarding what has truth and meaning not so much in itself as for the potential believer.

> To accept the kerygma means to recognize Jesus Christ as my Lord, as my Master. But, we must bear in mind, faith as acceptance of the kerygma is not only the recognition of a factually accepted message — in other words, the belief that a communication is true; at the same time it is acquiescence in a personal relation with Christ, the Kyrios. Indeed, the basic error of many analyses of the biblical concept of faith is that they have ignored this totalitarian character of the "acceptance of the kerygma." From the correct observation that, for Paul, "believe" generally means the acceptance of the message of salvation, the incorrect conclusion is drawn that this assent is simply an intellectual acceptance of truth. Thus E. Tobac describes the "acceptance of the Gospel" and the "reception of the preaching of the Apostles" as an "intellectual element" in the Pauline concept of faith. Whereas, in Bultmann's words, "Man, who in faith assents to the kerygma, thereby acknowledges this history (the life, death, and resurrection of Jesus Christ) as having taken place for him" (Hermann).

The act of Christian faith, then, is a decision not only that the gospel is "for real," but "for me."

Ratifying Christian Faith

Christian faith takes root only in a framework of freedom. The potential believer must be free to face every aspect of his

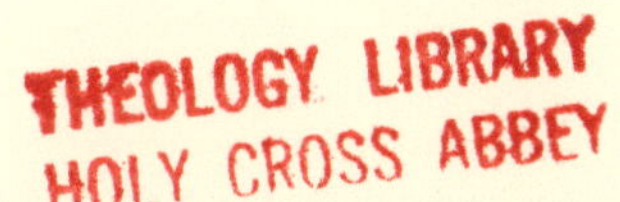

projected decision. Coercion will never produce genuine Christian faith.

This has always been acknowledged in the case of adult conversion. What has seldom been stressed is that freedom is also required for ratifying Christian faith born of childhood baptism and training.

Organic to Christian faith, no matter what the circumstances of its origin, is the right of "faith crisis." Like other moments of truth, Christian faith is born of uncertainty. Above all, it is born of time.

> There are realities that cannot be permanently grasped by a single effort. For example, one cannot determine so as to be ready for a decision whether one loves a person, after a single encounter and a subsequent analysis of the total impressions. . . . Thus it is not possible to "accept" in a single act the assertions of New Testament preaching about the salvific significance of Christ. . . . If one wants to "believe" the New Testament assertions concerning Christ as the indispensable salvation figure, one must rather confront that message and understanding basic to it with one's own potential of experience; one must *taste* in one's own life that this interpretation of the real "concerns me." Only thus is possible the inner evidence that leads to a reasoned decision of conscience. But this process takes some time, and therefore must not be confused with a purely intellectual admission that a thing is true (Hermann).

Ordinarily initial faith will be weak and hesitant, and it need not be otherwise. Nowhere do the gospels show Jesus expecting that initial faith be perfect.

> At first Jesus was satisfied with faith in the powers of healing invested in him, in the presence of God perceptible in his person. He was able to use such belief as a starting-point for Messianic faith, because healings, the driving out of evil spirits and other miracles forced the question of Messiahship to be raised. . . . Clearly faith, in these instances . . . entailed recognition even if as yet uninformed and immature of the religious significance of Jesus' person and work. It was just this recognition that Jesus wanted to develop further, as he had in the disciples . . . (Schnackenburg).

To be sure, Christian faith is not to be left immature. Neither is it to be imprudently exposed to further weakening. Ordinarily, however, it will be more tentative than tenacious in the beginning; and in great part this is due to the process of its emergence.

As a product of choice, Christian faith has a necessary prelude, a personal assessing of reasons for and against the choice. These reasons are external and internal.

External reasons are many and various, running a gamut from the historical reliability of the evangelists to the experienced reliability of one's parents. Vatican Council I suggested that the most telling of these is the fact of the Church's survival.

Internal reasons are perceptions of personal meaning and value in believing as a Christian. The realization that Christ has significance for one's own life, that faith will "work" in one's own case, is the most convincing of these.

Wending one's way to Christian belief through this maze of conflicting reasons can be considerably unsettling. For the maturing person faced with ratifying his childhood faith it frequently is. His problem is that of shifting the basis of his faith from the word of his parents and teachers to his own personal insights. Unraveling the essentials of Christian faith from the web of accidentals so typical of early religious training is an additional complication. The scene is that of a believer in search of "grounds" for his faith and for the authentic object of Christian faith. Religious and moral commitments suddenly loom too significant for previous assurances and explanations.

The ensuing "crisis" or even "loss" of faith, however, must never be identified with sin against faith — something altogether different. Rather than censure, what the perplexed believer needs is freedom and time, encouragement and trust. Since no one can supply faith for him, he must be allowed — even when prodded — to resolve his perplexity on his own.

Of course all is well, faithwise, with those who follow their conscience. Conscience, moreover, does not necessarily oblige to Christian faith, even in the case of one baptized. Only when all due conditions are verified, one of which is personal conviction, is one obliged to Christian faith. Though the *Declaration on Religious Freedom* says much that pertains to this, Vatican II's *Constitution on the Church* (16) has an especially applicable statement:

> Those also can attain to everlasting salvation who through no fault of their own do not know the gospel of Christ or His Church, yet sincerely seek God and, moved by grace, strive by their deeds to do His will as it is known to them through the dictates of conscience. Nor does divine Providence deny the help necessary for salvation to those who, without blame on their part, have not yet arrived at an explicit knowledge of God, but who strive to live a good life thanks to His grace.

If to their perplexity immature Christians bring a willingness to embrace Christ and the things of Christ as the matter clarifies in their mind, all is well, no matter how suspended or lost their Christian faith. Lacking this willingness, of course, the same cannot be said.

Finally, even a confirmed believer will never be able fully to explain the fact of his faith. Underlying all the internal and external factors of Christian faith is the unexplainable gift of God's grace — "No one knows the Father except the Son and those to whom the Son wills to reveal him; and no one comes to the Son except that the Father draw him." The initiative of the potential believer and of those helping him consists solely of so arranging things, internally and externally, that the drawing power of the Father and the word of the Son can come through. Prayer, Christian willingness, and encouragement are the main arrangements here. Beyond this, Christian faith and its development surpass human management.

Ultimately, then, Christian faith is a mystery, in its object, act, and ratification. Though begging for explanation — for theology — its secret will never be fully tapped.

Readings

Cirne-Lima, Carlos, *Personal Faith* (New York: Herder & Herder, 1965).

Hermann, Ingo, *The Experience of Faith* (New York: Kenedy, 1966).

Schnackenburg, Rudolph, *The Moral Teaching of the New Testament* (New York: Herder & Herder, 1965).

THEOLOGY

In Relation to Revelation and Faith

Unlike revelation and faith which are wholly or partly the product of God's saving activity, Christian theology is wholly the product of man's initiative. Christian theology begs, therefore, for an evaluation quite other than that due revelation and faith.

This point has to be stressed. "Crises of faith" are often directly the result of assigning Christian theology an undue significance. Only in a rudimentary and restricted sense is Christian theology identical with revelation and faith, a sense rarely verified. Doubtless it is verified in the word of Christ, in the statements on the Christian mysteries given by the apostles, and in the dogmas of the Church.

In these instances statement and revealed Reality coincide, even absolutely. In each case, however, a third factor is in evidence. The statements of Christ and the apostles indicate the influence of the "revealing Spirit," and are thus part of revelation itself. When committed to writing they embody "inspiration." With the Church's dogmas "infallibility" is at work. Here, then, we deal with Christian theology in a special sense, in the rudimentary and restricted sense of *stated revelation*. In the usual and technical sense Christian theology is something different.

Christian Theology in the Technical Sense

To be sure, the aim of Christian theology is always to be identical with what is revealed and believed, in terms of knowledge and understanding. It aims at being *explained revelation*, its time-honored definition, given by St. Anselm, being "the faith under analysis."

Aim and achievement, however, are two different things. As a human effort to analyze the mysteries of revelation and faith, Christian theology never wholly fulfills its ambition. For one thing, its subject matter defies complete analysis. There are aspects of God's life and love disclosed in revelation that completely surpass human comprehension — "mysteries" in the strict sense. Even the "naturally knowable" aspects of his life and love which revelation verifies are in great part impenetrable.

Of more current interest is the realization that man himself does not long remain in the same theological "situation"; he continually approaches the study of revelation from a different perspective. At least he should if he is intellectually alive. And what is true of the individual in this respect holds also for the entire Church.

This continual shifting of perspective is precisely what gives Christian theology a history. The New Testament indicates that from year to year within the apostolic community the understanding of revelation shifted. The Church fathers indicate this even more graphically: the problems they faced, the questions they asked, the examples they developed — all these served to give their theology a different hue than that of the apostles. Similarly, contemporary theology is of a different flavor than that of recent centuries.

The point is that, theology-wise, the last word on the understanding of revelation is never said. No explanation of what is revealed and believed is *absolutely* final, which is true, in a sense, even of those explanations which the Church affirms as dogmas.

These latter, of course, do embody an objective and unerring insight into some aspect of revelation. Nonetheless, they can always be seen from a different perspective, they can always be brought into a richer synthesis with later developments: unto fuller understanding and better explanation.

Rarely, though, does theological opinion win the stature of dogma, and except when it does it remains opinion and nothing more. To presume its dogmatic or infallible character is a great mistake, a temptation strongly to be resisted. The existence of dogma is to be proved, not presumed.

Deserving of emphasis, then, is the realization that whereas faith is a product of choice, Christian theology is a product of understanding. A theological position rests on reason, logic, and argumentation; it is to be retained or rejected solely in proportion to its strength, clearness, and orthodoxy.

As the subject of faith, Christ is a *constant*; as the subject of explanation he is a *variable*. And the same is to be said of the many mysteries he embodies and substantiates. Authentic believers must never let themselves be troubled by the essentially fluid character of theological understanding.

At this point theologians of the recent past have sought stability by advocating that the unanimous or common opinion of theologians on some article of faith provides a "semi-infallible" indication of what that article means.

Contemporary theologians find no fault with this. They are quick to note, though, that unanimity among theologians is not easy to come by. They insist, moreover, that unanimity cannot be measured solely in terms of one "school" of theology, whether Jesuit, Dominican, Franciscan, "new" or "old," no matter how celebrated or agreed its participants. They are also more sensitive than their earlier colleagues to the variations on the same theme to be found among Catholic, non-Catholic, and even non-Christian thinkers, variations begging for honest comparison and evalution in the process of forming unanimous or common opinion.

In a word, contemporary theologians insist that, like dogmas, the existence of unanimous or common theological opinion is to be proved, not presumed. Lacking proof, they hold themselves and the faithful only to the law of orthodoxy, not to that of alleged "semi-infallibility."

Three Faces of Theology

Because revelation is supremely knowable and glimpses of its meaning are really attainable, Christian theology is extremely important and worthwhile. In the recent past theology's worth was mainly seen as culminating in the drawing from revelation hidden or unsuspected truths. It was also esteemed as an invaluable tool for tracing the statements of the Church back to Scripture and Tradition.

Without denying the merits of that estimate, contemporary theologians envision Christian theology more as a direct grappling with Scripture and Tradition for the sake of judging the statements of the Church. Too preoccupied with what is obvious in revelation, they also see little place in theology for the academic pleasantry of deducing revelation's more abstract secrets.

What is going on in the field of theology today deals mainly with what is called positive theology, as distinct from systematic and pastoral theology. The latter, of course, is undergoing conscientious development, and systematic theology, never far from where the action is, is also stirring. The times, however, belong to positive theology, and it has been thus for well over a century.

The technical terms, positive, systematic, and pastoral, refer to three aspects or "faces" of the overall task of theology. In a masterful article on the matter, John Thornhill, S.M., has described each of these and its relationship to theology as a whole. His thesis is that a full theology must feature all three; failing this, theology as a whole or any particular theological explanation remains unfinished.

By positive theology is meant the study of the "sources" of theology for the sake of grasping with certainty the full range of the Church's faith. The sources in question are usually the written records of the Church, the reflections of her chief theologians, and Christian monuments such as burial inscriptions, liturgical art and architecture, festive and other customs. Each of these sources witnesses in different ways to aspects of the Church's faith.

Sources vigorously studied today are the Scriptures, the writings of the Church fathers, and the liturgy. Interest in a scientific study of these dates to the early past century, and this more than anything else led to Vatican II and the current renewal of theology.

Other sources are also being studied, as they always have been. Chief among these are statements of the *magisterium*, that is, of the Church's official teachers: popes (and Curia), councils, and bishops.

In recent centuries the study of magisterial documents had become the main preoccupation of positive theology. The result of this was that not a few in the Church regarded theology as little more than a commentary on Henricus Denzinger's nineteenth-century collection of ecclesiastical statements.

In our own day Denzinger theology has become a dirty word. This, of course, is not entirely just, since theology must ever begin and end with the magisterium. What is seen more clearly today, however, is that the magisterium also proclaims its mind in sources other than those of the Denzinger collection. The Bible and liturgy are two outstanding cases in point.

Today positive theology has a broader task than that assigned it in recent centuries. To the study of later developments has been added the rediscovering of the doctrinal traditions that predate the sixteenth-century Council of Trent. In too many instances after that council magisterial declarations were too limited in scope to reflect the total faith of the Church. Even prior to Trent this same limitation is often to be met with.

In this respect the statements of Vatican II are wholly unique in the annals of magisterial pronouncements. Its documents aimed simply at stating the Church's faith rather than arguing isolated installments of it. For the first time, one might say, positive theology was helped rather than hindered by solemn magisterial teachings. Its overall objective of locating all points of the Church's faith was greatly facilitated.

Systematic theology begins, as it were, where positive theology ends. The believing mind seeks to penetrate the message of revelation for its meaning and relationship to things of human experience. Systematic theology, thus, is the translating of revelation into human ideas and words as far as this is possible.

For all that this effort threatens to wring from revelation its warm, personal attractiveness, systematic theology provides an indispensable service for the Church. It takes revelation "out of the clouds," as it were, and roots it in man's experience and understanding of his world. Faith cannot long endure as an assent to what has no clear and certain bearing on one's real self and world. Grasping for that bearing makes faith intelligent rather than mystical or merely pious. Unless one's faith also makes sense, a person will cling to it in an unmanly way or soon drop it as something unmanly.

At the present time systematic theology is seemingly overwhelmed with the wealth of "new" data that positive theology has unearthed in the older tradition. Only slowly can this mass of information be examined and translated into an orderly program of meaning for modern man. Systematic theology, however, is on the threshold of a truly remarkable future. The decades ahead will see countless instances of the Church's understanding being enriched by the insights of systematic theologians. Illustrations of these can already be cited, as will be seen in several of the following chapters.

Pastoral theology is concerned with the communicating and living of the conclusions of positive and systematic theology. Its special area of emphasis is the relationship between revelation and life.

Positive theology concentrates as much on the persons who are to live the faith as on the faith itself considered as a way of life. It studies all that conditions modern man for and against life in Christ. It seeks to understand not only for the sake of initiating faith, but to bring life in faith to fullness, both in individuals and in the whole body of the Church. It aims also at guiding believers toward a genuinely Christian relationship with and participation in the world.

In this latter respect, pastoral theology is assisted today by a mood pervading both positive and systematic theology, namely, the desire to understand more clearly not only the message of revelation in itself, but all things in the light of that message. Emphasized today is the study of everything human, everything created, in the light of the gospel. Vatican II's *Constitution on the Church in the Modern World* is a good example of this emphasis; so too the papers read by leading theologians at Notre Dame and Toronto in 1966 and 1967, respectively.

Theology, therefore, tends today to be a study of man and the world for the sake of Christ. In recent centuries it tended to be something else: a study of Christ for the sake of man and the world. Both moods, ultimately, are necessary for a complete theology. The mood today, though, is not wholly unlike that which predominated in the heart of Christ himself.

Readings

Miller, John H., C.S.C., *Vatican II: An Interfaith Appraisal* (South Bend, Ind.: University of Notre Dame Press, 1966).

Schillebeeckx, Edward, O.P., *Revelation and Theology* (New York: Sheed & Ward, 1967).

Thornhill, John, S.M., "Toward An Integral Theology," *Theological Studies*, June, 1963.

Wolf, Donald, S.J., and Schall, James V., S.J. (eds.), *Current Trends in Theology* (Garden City, N. Y.: Doubleday & Co., 1965).

DOCTRINE

If it is imperative to distinguish faith and theology, it is equally necessary to make some distinctions regarding doctrine. Attaching the name "Catholic Doctrine" to some idea gives many people a feeling of security. It gives many others a feeling of uneasiness.

"Catholic Doctrine" is a very general notion. It refers to what expresses in some way the thought of the Church. It does not say in what way the Church's mind is thus expressed. There are many ways in which the Church says what she thinks.

Some Necessary Distinctions

"Catholic Doctrine" has two meanings, one popular, the other technical. Popularly, "Catholic Doctrine" means whatever pertains to the Catholic Church's overall position on matters divine and human. Catechisms and religion textbooks usually spell this out in detail. What they present under the heading "Catholic Doctrine" is a collection of dogmas, common teachings, preferred opinions, organizational structures, laws, and practices — a totality of ideas embodying an overview of the entire life and outlook of the Church.

Applying the term "Catholic Doctrine" to this totality has the advantage of identifying each and all the ingredients of the total Catholic viewpoint on matters theological, ecclesiastical, and temporal. A disadvantage is that it tends to confuse, in trained and untrained minds alike, certainty and opinion, dogma and prudential teaching, divine and human law, faith and theology, custom and revelation, thought and obedience.

Such is the disadvantage of this popular use of the term that it tends to shackle rather than liberate the children of God. It tends inevitably to verify what Drinkwater concurs in calling the paralysis of "creeping infallibility." It promotes what Rudolph

Schnackenburg identifies as one of the major misconceptions that Jesus tried to correct, namely, "the Jewish view that every precept, great or small, whether it concerned the heart or external matters, was equally binding in obedience, because it was 'a prescription of the King of Kings.'"

Technically, "Catholic Doctrine" means *magisterial* doctrine. In recent centuries this has meant the teachings set forth in the official documents of the Roman See and diocesan chanceries. Dogmas and prudential or authentic teachings are classical examples of this notion of "Catholic Doctrine." The idea here is that of *official* teaching set forth in *official* documents by *official* teachers of the Church and in the name of the Church.

Today it is emphasized that the teaching office (magisterium) of the Church expresses itself in other ways than the official documents so familiar since the Council of Trent. Scripture and liturgy illustrate two of these ways. More fluid than official documents, less determined as to meaning and due response, these further ways of teaching are nonetheless valid and orthodox expressions of the mind of the Church.

Another thing emphasized today is that "Catholic Doctrine" does not always originate with the magisterium. At times it comes directly from the insights of theologians. It may even arise from the faith or understanding of the faithful at large. Many of the perceptions endorsed by the bishops at Vatican II did not originate with the bishops, and developments since the Council have not all been the work of bishops. The American bishops' pastoral on *The Church in Our Day* illustrates the historical truth of this in its section on the *Laity*.

A Critical Problem

A critical problem today centers on identifying "Catholic Doctrine." Doubtless the endorsement of the magisterium gives an objective and universal certainty that new insights and developments are "Catholic Doctrine." This endorsement, however, does not of itself bestow orthodoxy. Insights and developments are orthodox or not of themselves, and those holding them can be personally certain of their orthodoxy long before the judgment of the magisterium.

What to do? In recent centuries personal certainty has been discounted in favor of objective and universal standards of certainty. This has meant waiting on the judgment of the hierarchy. Today this procedure seems inadequate, both for the good of individuals and of the Church as a whole. It is thought insufficient today to tell individuals or groups to keep thinking but to wait before teaching or acting. The reason is that even the hierarchy has to learn, has to be taught.

More orthodox than waiting is a conscientious applying of the traditional "norms for the discerning of spirits." Developed in the interest of the spiritual life, these norms apply with slight modification to the intellectual and theological life as well.

Many things are involved here. Joseph De Guibert's *Theology of the Spiritual Life* gives some idea of these, docility, humility, peacefulness, and patience being among them. A fundamental factor is a willingness constantly to compare one's insights or conclusions with the sound tradition of the Church. The American bishops add that one's thinking must always refer to the community, not just to oneself.

Always one's insights must concur with magisterial doctrine if they are to qualify as "Catholic Doctrine." This does not mean that the magisterial doctrine applicable to the case must be of recent vintage. Even magisterial statements must harmonize with the original faith and tradition of the Church.

Two things may be concluded here. First, "Catholic Doctrine" is partly a matter of personal judgment and partly a matter of magisterial judgment. Second, the Church must adjust to conscience as a standard of orthodoxy as it has adjusted to the magisterium as such a standard.

Obviously the Church needs the objective and universal certainty that only the magisterium can provide. Just as obviously it needs the responsible convictions of individuals and groups. What it does not need is a pattern of thinking that these two areas are rigidly separate and inevitably antagonistic.

Contending always with its mystery, the Church as a whole — bishops, theologians, and laity — must constantly be in search of its ever more adequate understanding. "Catholic Doctrine" should develop and clarify as a unified enterprise of the entire Church.

Infallibility

Part of today's problem hinges on the nature and place of infallibility in the Church.

Since Vatican Council I, a century ago, infallibility has been explained almost exclusively in terms of the magisterium. That Council defined papal infallibility and clarified under what conditions bishops teach infallibly. The Pope was declared infallible when teaching *ex cathedra*, that is, when addressing the entire Church, with the fullness of his apostolic authority, on a matter pertaining to faith or morals, and binding all the faithful to his conclusion(s). Bishops were said to be infallible when teaching in ecumenical council or unanimously throughout the world.

Little or no attention has been paid since Vatican I to the extremely important truth that papal infallibility is part of the infallibility possessed by the entire Church. Another point, therefore, never as yet fully clarified is the common teaching of theologians that infallibility takes expression also in the belief of the faithful.

Prominent today is the awareness that there is more at work in the Church than a magisterium endowed with special prerogatives. Such a magisterium there certainly is, but there is also the body of the faithful sharing in due measure in the same teaching mission and prerogatives as the magisterium. And this sharing is misconceived if understood wholly as something passive.

A point begging for understanding in the Church today is that the magisterium does not so much "formulate" the Church's faith and understanding as bears official witness to it. This implies that the magisterium itself must learn or discover the mind of the Church. Scholars play a vital role here, as the *periti* did at Vatican II, but so do the faithful at large. Ideally, bishops take to their magisterial meetings the "pooled" thinking of all their subjects. A thinking and vocal laity is an essential ingredient of a living Church.

Another point deserving of serious attention is the traditional understanding that infallibility is more a negative than a positive influence. Its effect is not to inform the Church, but simply to keep it from making profound doctrinal or disciplinary mistakes.

What this means in practice is that infallibility is more a "happening" than something consciously invoked. The Church knows less than more about when or how infallibility works. And never has it been suggested that infallibility is a substitute for intellectual enterprise and responsibility.

When it comes to theology, therefore — and even dogmas are theology — the Church must rely on her human wits rather than on any measurable divine intervention. She must gather information from whatever sources she can and make up her own mind regarding it. And all in the Church must understand that the same influence that mysteriously protects the judgment of the magisterium from error is also at work in those who supply the information for that judgment. In fact, among the latter that protective influence may well be more tangible and accelerated.

Dogmatic Teachings

That the Church is definitely infallible in her dogmatic teachings deserves emphasis today. In an era of doctrinal renewal ambiguity can easily arise on this score. It seems advisable, therefore, to make this very fundamental point: dogmas represent or state insights of the Church into the mystery of God's revelation that are unerringly and unchangeably correct.

Dogmas are formulated, nonetheless, only in the light of the Church's understanding at any given moment of her history. Never do they tell the whole or final story of the Church's understanding of any point of her faith. Neither do they escape the disadvantages of history. Canon Drinkwater likens a dogma to a snowball: the longer one rolls it the more foreign matter it collects. To get at the real meaning of its original insight the Church must periodically remove from her dogmas all the nonessential and misleading notions that have come to surround them with the passing of time. Though dogmas embody an objective and unerring insight into the meaning of revelation, they do not say the last word on that insight. No dogma will ever be reversed, but none will long go without further refinement and clarification.

The dogma that Christ is one Person in two natures is a case in point. When finally clarified at Chalcedon, in 451, after the earlier ambiguities of Ephesus, in 431, and Nicaea, in 325, the heart of the insight was little more than that Jesus is "one Thing, but also two things: divine and human, God and man" (Bowman). *Person* and *Nature* had conflicting meanings in East and West, and little of their real depth was grasped at the time.

Even for St. Thomas, eight centuries later, *Nature* had more meaning than *Person*, and thus the dogma received at his hands a one-sided treatment. Today, on the other hand, the study of the idea *Person* has opened vistas of understanding not even suspected before. Were a council to "explain" Christ today, its statement, though verbally faithful to Chalcedon and St. Thomas, could be notably richer and more balanced.

Dogmas call for an assent of genuine faith: they are to be held as true by reason of the divine revelation they express. Obviously they are not things to be treated casually. For this reason the Church owes it to herself clearly to identify her dogmas. Indiscriminately to apply that term to teachings or "positions" of the Church helps no one. A point of "Catholic Doctrine" must be proven, not presumed, to be a dogmatic teaching.

Dogmas are rather easily identifiable when stemming from a papal definition or an ecumenical council. It is less easy to discover them on the basis of the unanimous teaching of bishops throughout the world. In either event, though, they express but limited aspects of the faith of the Church, and must, therefore, be neither identified with the whole of the Church's faith nor with the whole of "Catholic Doctrine" regarding the faith.

Readings

Abbott & Gallagher (eds.), *Dogmatic Constitution on Divine Revelation*, in *The Documents of Vatican II* (New York: Guild Press, 1966).

The Church in Our Day, Pastoral of the American Bishops (Washington, D. C.: U. S. Catholic Conference, 1968).

De Guibert, Joseph, S.J., *The Theology of the Spiritual Life* (New York: Sheed & Ward, 1953), Chap. 1–3, Part 3.

Drinkwater, F. H., *Birth Control and Natural Law* (Baltimore: Helicon, 1965).

Powell, John, S.J., *The Mystery of the Church* (Milwaukee: Bruce, 1967).

Schillebeeckx, Edward, O.P., *Revelation and Theology* (New York: Sheed & Ward, 1967), Vol. 1.

Maguire, Daniel C., "Moral Absolutes and the Magisterium," in *Absolutes in Moral Theology?* ed. by Charles Curran (Washington, D.C.: Corpus Books, 1968), pp. 57–107.

DIRECTIVES

Not all "Catholic Doctrine" is infallible. A great deal of it certainly is not. Neither is it all exclusively concerned with thought and understanding. Much of it looks directly to behavior.

As a rule the magisterium fulfills its teaching and guiding mission through "provisional" judgments. These take the form of *authentic teachings* or *disciplinary decrees*, which for practical purposes can be gathered together under the heading *prudential directives*. Unlike dogmas, these directives represent only what seems here and now to the mind of the magisterium as most in keeping with Christian and/or human values.

Prudential Directives

First to be noted about prudential directives is that they do not represent a definitive judgment of the Church. Rather, they enunciate a magisterial "opinion" or "position" regarding a practical question of thought or behavior.

Second, prudential directives look to the common good. They are not "private replies" or "precepts," both of which in technical language look wholly to the instruction or guidance of an individual. Prudential directives are communal in scope. They represent what in the judgment of the magisterium is the wiser and more prudent course for a community to follow. The community in question may be the entire Church or a group within the Church. At times their scope envisions even the whole of mankind, though in these instances their acceptance and following is obviously only a duty for those who believe in the Church.

What is the duty these directives impose? Unlike dogmas, they do not call for a response of strict faith. Theologians name the response due them *religious assent,* and traditionally explain this as a reverential inner acceptance more genuine than a mere "obsequious silence."

In speaking thus theologians primarily have in mind *prudential teachings*, directives that look to a way of thinking. Pius XII's encyclical *Humani Generis* is a classical case in point, wherein a "position" was taken on evolution and other contemporary doctrinal questions. Pope Paul's *Progressio Populorum*, which explains Christian morality in relation to underdeveloped nations, is another example. Numerous pastoral letters of bishops — Suhard, Shehan, De Smedt — could also be cited.

What is said of prudential teachings, however, applies equally to *disciplinary decrees*. What needs to be stressed, in other words, is the element of *obedience* in religious assent. Though it is true that the Church asks the faithful to accept her "provisional" *thinking* on practical questions, with her prudential directives she is mainly asking the faithful to act upon that thinking. Teachers are asked to teach the "stand" of the Church; scholars are asked to direct their research by that stand; the faithful at large are asked to make their decisions in light of that stand.

Rather than weakening the authority of prudential directives, emphasizing their appeal to obedience seems precisely to establish their strength. It will only be through obedience that the prudence of these directives will be concretely implemented. Nothing is really accomplished by asking people *only* to think in a particular way. On the other hand, one cannot long obey the Church without a willingness to think with the Church. It is for the sake of acting, of obeying, therefore, that the thought-basis of the directive is to be accepted.

Prudential directives do not close the door to further thought, or even to efforts to have them changed. Unlike dogmas, they are neither infallible nor unchangeable. They represent a choice among several possible approaches. Information available to the Church is not sufficient to make the choice final; it only makes it seem prudent. Further information will substantiate or negate the wisdom of that choice. But further information will only be forthcoming and effective if the Church as a whole, and the magisterium in particular, continue to study and evaluate the matter.

Relative to this, prudential directives carry no guarantee as to their correctness, opportuneness, or necessity. There is no guarantee that they will be more advantageous than detrimental. Their only guarantee — which is considerable — is that if accepted and followed salvation will not be jeopardized.

Limitations

Guaranteeing that salvation will not be jeopardized is not, of course, the same as saying that the Christian life will positively be promoted to the highest degree. Neither is it to say that every individual Christian will reap the greatest spiritual profit from the stand taken by the Church. Individuals may well suffer spiritual loss as a result of this stand, and the Church itself may be short-changed as far as overall growth is concerned. The reason for this may be nothing but human weakness, but damage can result nonetheless.

Accepting and following prudential directives is mainly, then, a serving of the salvation of the community. And it is this service, this sacrifice of self, that the Church is asking of the faithful when it takes a prudential position. Surely, responding to this will be of spiritual benefit to the individual. It is unreal to think, however, that in every case, and in every way, an individual will come off the better for it. Situations can be envisioned in which the individual will come off the worse, even if only because of his own weakness, whether in terms of health, happiness, or faith.

It is a good question, therefore, as to how far an individual is bound to a prudential position which, while aiming at the common good, works an undermining of individual well-being. Do prudential directives have limitations, in other words? Do they oblige the whole community without restriction to religious assent and obedience, and do they allow for individual exceptions?

Two things suggest that these questions can be answered in the affirmative, and a third supports this conclusion.

The first of these is the communal scope of prudential directives. These directives aim at securing the well-being of a community. Precisely because of this they lay claim to the sacrificial loyalties of the individual.

Not every individual exception, however, threatens the achieving of that aim. This is especially the case where an exception would concern mere private or secret behavior. If privacy be maintained, and the person(s) involved accept the responsibility of secrecy, the community's well-being would not be threatened by the exception. It could, therefore, be allowed.

The second factor of significance is the primacy of obedience in the obligation imposed by prudential directives. These directives do not impose mere thought, but certain expressions of thought. They require certain actions related to a stipulated line of thought.

What regulates activity, however, has the nature of law, and law admits of well-defined exceptions. An individual is not obliged to a Church law, for example, when obedience works a personal disadvantage comparable in seriousness to what the law aims to secure. Especially is he not obliged when in the face of such a disadvantage his being excused would not undermine the public well-being of the Church. And this is true even if the only way he can offset that disadvantage is by means of an action which in other circumstances might be of disadvantage to the community. In the circumstances that prevail, therefore, the exception could be allowed.

Supportive of this conclusion is the long-established policy of allowing exceptions to Church laws, a policy that has not worked to any major disadvantage for the Church. Though prudential directives are not exactly laws, their communal scope and obligation to obedience make them greatly akin to laws. In virtue of this, one could safely predict that allowing exceptions to them according to norms pertaining to laws would work no great disadvantage for the Church.

Contraception

What does this mean in practice? An illustration can be found in the Church's prudential directive prohibiting contraception.

First, a word on this illustration. That the prohibition of contraception and the doctrinal position underlying it is a prudential directive follows from two considerations. The first is that the vast majority of theologians do not regard it as a dogmatic teaching. The second is that John R. Noonan has convincingly shown that whereas the traditional teaching of the Church clearly opposes such contraception as contradicts the essential values of marriage, it does not clearly close the door to the possible acceptability of contraception compatible with those values, namely, *responsible* contraception. Pope Paul has prohibited the latter, and in the name of the traditional teaching, but prudentially, not definitively.

Accompanying this stand is a way of thinking and acting wholly meant for the well-being of the Church and mankind. Its aim is to insure the due relationship between procreative and personal values in marriage, both as to their understanding and pursuit. Lacking a more adequate doctrinal understanding, the magisterium has judged that none other than the traditional understanding is fully secure. Thus all the faithful, especially those who are married, have been asked to keep their consciences formed according to the traditional understanding and norms.

In an individual case this way of thinking and acting may well be to the serious detriment of a couple. Further pregnancies may be physically, psychologically, or economically inadvisable, even morally impossible. Approved methods of conception control may be unworkable, and the reason may be none other than personal weakness, even of a moral and religious kind. In the real situation the traditional line of thought and practice may be working to the deep and genuine suffering of the person(s), a marriage, children, or even faith.

Faced with the likely loss of the very values that the prudential directive aims to secure for the community, or with the loss of other values equally important, the couple in question seems justified in concluding that the ingredients of a legitimate exception to that directive are present. For one thing, their acting to the contrary, if wholly private, would not be to the prejudice of the community. For another, their own critical needs justify their preferring their own well-being to the nonthreatened well-being of the community. Valid grounds for judging themselves an exception to the rule enjoined by Pope Paul's encyclical of 1968 seem unquestionably, therefore, to be verified. Always, of course, the willingness to be guided by further clarifications on the part of the magisterium must be kept alive.

Shortcomings

Prudential directives have many inherent shortcomings. Not the least of these is that they are "provisional" rather than definitive decisions. They rest on only partial information, and give nothing like the certainty of dogma. This fact alone makes each of them even more of a "hard saying" than an infallible proclamation.

Karl Rahner is of the opinion that in the future these short-comings will be increased rather than lessened. Practical questions, he says, whether of doctrine or practice, will continue to become more complicated. Tentative solutions will become progressively more unrealistic. Instead, prudential directives will have to busy themselves with principles and with the values that any solution will have to retain. This will place special responsibilities on both the magisterium and the faithful. And Peter Chirico has written recently in a similar vein, stressing that even in the case of practical decisions some values have to be preferred over others in spite of the fact that in other circumstances this preference would be unjustified: a person, in other words, is unable always to pursue every value that he is committed to pursue as a man and a Christian.

In spite of their shortcomings, however, prudential directives remain the one means through which the good of the Church and mankind is most adequately insured. As often as not, too, they are the main means through which the Church's under-standing develops.

The magisterium issues these in the name of Christ, and pro-vides through them a service of incalculable love toward both Church and world. They deserve the greatest respect on the part of the faithful, for all that they pose one of the most difficult of Christian burdens. Being practical interventions, prudential direc-tives should ideally be rare and reluctantly given. Guidance, care, and responsibility, however, whether in Church, state, or home, cannot long have practical meaning unless they issue in decisions and directives.

Readings

The Church in Our Day, American Bishops' Pastoral (Washington, D. C.: U. S. Catholic Conference, 1968).

Curran, Charles, ed., Absolutes in Moral Theology? (Washington, D.C.: Corpus Books, 1968).

Ford, John, S.J., and Kelly, Gerald, S.J., Contemporary Moral The-ology (Westminster, Md.: Newman, 1958), Vol 1, Chap. 1–3.

Noonan, John R., Contraception: A History of its Treatment by the Catholic Theologians and Canonists (Cambridge, Mass.: Harvard University Press, 1965).

Pope Paul VI, *Humanae Vitae*, July 29, 1968.

Quade, Quentin L., and Rhodes, James M., "What Can the Church Demand?" *The Catholic World*, December, 1966, pp. 162–169.

Rahner, Karl, S.J., *The Christian of the Future* (New York: Herder & Herder, 1967).

Theological Studies, June, 1967, articles by Milhaven and Casey, Dupre and Chirico on changing trends in moral theory and directives.

PART THREE

Central Doctrines

INCARNATION

How can Jesus be both God and man? This is the perennial question central to Christian thought. From the beginning it has taxed and tantalized Christian thinkers, and as they have answered so has fared the Christian community. It has always been and always will be the quality of the Church's understanding of the incarnation that mainly determines the quality of her understanding of all other things, herself included.

Since God is not known directly, but only through the things that signify him, it is the human side of Christ that has always been the key to "explaining" the incarnation. This is verified in the history of theology, both recent and ancient; and it is no less true in contemporary theology. The differences that characterize contemporary theology on the incarnation rest ultimately on differences in the understanding of humanness.

Historical Developments

More clearly than the other evangelists, St. John identified the divine Person in Jesus. And he did this precisely by portraying the humanity of Jesus so realistically. The genius of the fourth Gospel is that conviction regarding the divinity of Christ rests firmly on conviction regarding his humanness.

By the time John wrote his Gospel and letters things had changed considerably for the early Christians. It was then some seventy years since Jesus had passed from the scene, at least visually. No longer just a Jewish community in Israel, the Church had spread throughout the Near East and into the West. It was peopled by Jews, Greeks, and Romans.

In order to speak meaningfully to this diversity of peoples, the apostles began early to translate both Christ's teachings and their own belief in him into non-Jewish ideas and terms. They had to anticipate questions put to them by their non-Jewish hearers and converts, and they had to respond to these. St. Paul's letters clearly illustrate this, and, if examined closely, so does St. Luke's Gospel.

St. John's Gospel and letters are another case in point. By the year A.D. 100, when he wrote, the first major misunderstanding of Jesus' identity had arisen. A group of converts was maintaining that Jesus had only *seemed* to be human: he is the Son of God, but not really man.

To this group, the *Docetists*, John answered: only because he is truly human can Jesus be known as truly God; only in and through his real humanity can the lines of his real Person be detected. "We believe it is the Word of Life that came among us because we have seen and heard him, have walked and talked with him, have eaten with him, and touched him."

In writing thus, St. John gave the Church its richest exposition on the divinity of Christ. And he did this by confirming the realness of Jesus' humanity.

Several things are to be noted here. One is an illustration of how doctrine developed in the Church from the beginning. Another is the clarifying of the Church's understanding of Jesus' identity. Closely related, neither should be missed.

Originally, the Church was concerned solely with proclaiming her own commitment to Christ, concentrating on such events and experiences as invited and supported sharing in that commitment. What she presented was the *kerygma*, the nucleus of her message set forth for the sake of inspiring conversion.

To the kerygma, following conversion, was added *catechesis*, that is, further instruction. For Jew and Gentile alike commitment to Christ had to be explained, reinforced, and expanded. Doubtless such questions as, "What exactly is it that we believe?" and "What reasons day by day support our faith?" were frequently put to the apostles. In response they examined their own faith in Christ ever more deeply and set forth the fruit of their thought clearly and strongly.

What we call *theology*, the systematic and organized study of each mystery of the faith, came only later. Like kerygma and catechesis, however, it arose in response to a new situation. As the Church continued to take in new members, to spread to new places, and to live its commitment through new years, it had to contend with different needs, interests, questions, thought-patterns, and languages. Each of these called for new approaches and emphases.

By the time St. John was writing it was no longer sufficient for the Church merely to show that Jesus had demonstrated himself the fulfillment of Israel's messianic prophecies. The Church had now a different audience, as it were, than Jews. Many of her hearers and converts now came from a wholly different cultural background. And for some of these accepting Jesus as God was one thing but as man quite another: they had been brought up to regard the human body as evil, as a sign and result of man's ancient sin.

Not only did St. John have to catechize regarding the divinity of Christ, therefore, but he had to explain that having a human body was not the result of some mythical sin. He had to put sin down to the power of choice rather than in the fact of human flesh, which was extremely important since many in his audience and many with whom they regularly rubbed shoulders were conditioned to think otherwise. They had been led to feel that whereas the mind is good the body is evil. Quite natural, therefore, was their conclusion that if Jesus is God his body cannot be real.

Two hundred years later another audience had yet a different problem with Jesus. The background of the *Arians* made it natural for them to see Jesus as an auxiliary or lower-level God. Their problem was not so much the humanity of Jesus as his Person. Actually, though, their preconceptions regarding the nature of God prevented their seeing in Christ's humanness all the signs of his real personal identity. In A.D. 325, the Council of Nicaea dealt with this, proclaiming Jesus to be *consubstantial* — separate but equal — with the Father.

A hundred years afterward the question was again different. This time it was a matter of keeping Jesus a unity. The *Nestorians* apparently had no problem either with Jesus as divine or Jesus as human; they could not see how he could be both at once.

Here, too, though, was a misunderstanding of humanness: as man is one while being both person and nature, so Jesus is one while being divine and human. The Council of Ephesus, in A.D. 431, had to explain that Christ and Jesus are not two Persons in wonderful harmony, but one Person standing in being in two ways: in one way that is divine, in another that is human.

Twenty years later, at the Council of Chalcedon, another installment of explanation was required. If Jesus is one Person, the *Monophysites* argued, his humanness is really not important. What really matters is that he stands in being in a divine way. In comparison with the divine, after all, anything human is of little significance: it is like a drop of water compared to the ocean.

To the council fathers of Chalcedon the facts were quite otherwise. Jesus is the Son of God, they proclaimed, but existing in the fullness of the human condition, sin excepted. He has "emptied" himself of the glory due his Person in order to affirm the dignity of his humanness. He came not to overwhelm humanity with his majesty, but to hint at his majesty through the goodness of his humanity. Here again, in new language, is the teaching of St. John.

Medieval Concerns

By the beginning of the Middle Ages most of the technical terms used even today in explaining the incarnation had been devised. This was one of the great contributions of the early ecumenical Councils. Surprisingly, though, these terms lacked unmistakable precision until the theologians of the twelfth and thirteenth centuries set their minds to work explaining them. Passionately devoted to precision, these thinkers aimed at explaining "nature" and "person" with such clarity as to render further misunderstandings of the incarnation quite impossible.

In the process they developed even further precisions. "Essence" and "existence" became technical ideas with reference to the incarnation. Of singular importance was the notion "subsistence," which came to represent the unique individuality of personal beings. Another term coined at the time was "hypostatic union," meaning the union of two natures in one Person. Though drawn from the early councils this became a key phrase in the medieval discussion.

In briefest summary, the basic theology of the incarnation according to the medievalists was this: Jesus is the Son of God uniting in his own Person two natures, one divine and the other human, the human nature having neither existence nor subsistence of its own, but deriving both being and personal individuality from the Son of God. And the name of this special union was "hypostatic," from the Greek word *hypostasis* meaning person.

Accustomed as we are today to different thought-patterns, it is perhaps difficult to see the precision in this. It seems more ambiguous than precise. On the other hand, we can surely agree that it is *technical*, and such it was meant to be. The great contribution of the medieval schoolmen was precisely a technicality of ideas and language, and theology has profited from it ever since.

But the medievalists also had other interests. One of these was the knowing process in Christ. In light of the hypostatic union they explained this as an interplay between three ways that Jesus knew things. The first of these was called *beatific*, and was much the same way of knowing as is experienced by the saints in glory, only in the case of Jesus it was much richer because of the altogether special intimacy between his human mind and the Son of God. The second way of knowing was called *infused*, which entailed a unique gift of knowledge bequeathed to his human mind for the sake of fulfilling his messianic mission. The third way was called *experiential*, and this was described as that common to all human minds, a way of knowing proper to Jesus by reason of his being fully human in all things but sin.

The medievalists seemingly had little difficulty in keeping these ways of knowing in harmony. On one level of his intelligence Jesus was seen as knowing all things; on another level messianic information; and on still another such things as he learned day by day and year by year from ordinary human experience. None of these levels apparently interfered with the others, and the lack of conflict was at once both a sign and a "proof" of his unique identity.

Recent And Contemporary Concerns

For all practical purposes the medieval theology of the incarnation has come down to the present day without alteration. There is, in a word, on this point no difference between recent and contemporary theology since there is nothing to qualify as "recent" theology on the make-up of Christ. Between the traditional theology and contemporary thought, however, there are several remarkable differences. These follow from the trend among contemporary theologians to take very seriously the fact that in Jesus the Son of God became fully human.

There is among contemporary theologians who discuss the incarnation what may be called a "kenotic" emphasis. The word derives from St. Paul's famous line to the Philippians (2:6–11) about Jesus "emptying" himself in the incarnation of the glory that was his as Son of God. So emphatic is this "emptying" theme with modern thinkers that they prefer not to deal with the Son's previous or eternal condition at all. They begin with the Jesus of the gospels, and attempt to explain only the incarnation that is historically portrayed there.

And first to be noted about this portrayal is the complete and consistent humanness of Jesus. Not that he is not divine; his divinity is surely part of the portrayal, since the Scriptures present Christ as he was believed in by the Church. But his divine identity is "hidden" or "emptied" in the complete humanness of Jesus. Even the Lord's miracles so followed the lines of his humanness that they were "signs" only to those who had already come to some belief in him through contact with his humanness.

Concentrating on what it means fully to be man, especially as this is diagnosed by modern philosophers, contemporary theologians find it difficult to accept the traditional explanation of Christ's knowing process, especially his knowing of himself, his self-consciousness. Beatific knowledge, they say, simply does not stand up with the fully human side of the incarnation, at least not until after the resurrection. Infused knowledge, maybe, since this is in harmony with high holiness, but beatific knowledge, no. It is experiential knowledge that most befits Jesus, which would extend to his understanding both of himself and his mission as well as to everything else pertaining to the real humanness of his life.

There is, of course, a profound problem in all of this, and it is not lost on these theologians. As Son of God Jesus was surely in possession of a divine self-consciousness; he knew his personal identity at all times. The question is, though, whether this means he knew everything, and whether, like the saints in glory, his consciousness of God flooded his spirit with fulfilling rapture.

To this question contemporary theologians answer no. In explanation they suggest that a distinction be made between beatific or fulfilling knowledge and divine knowledge that only gradually unfolds in the form of human understanding. Jesus' self-consciousness as Son of God, they suggest, is one thing; its being experienced in human form is another. We all know ourselves, our vocation, our surroundings, but gradually and ever more deeply. The process-side of knowing even ourselves is a feature of genuine humanness. It should not be thought otherwise with the incarnate Son of God. He knew himself as Son, and all that this implies, but in a human way. Only gradually did he grasp its ever deeper significance; gradually too he came to know his Father's will and the way this would be best fulfilled.

Jesus, therefore, is not God "in disguise." He is God become man. Only by seeing the fullness of his humanness, as St. John originally inferred, can we hope to see the fullness of his divine identity. To the extent that his humanness is unreal, to the same extent there is reason not to take him seriously. A faulty sign, especially of God, deserves to be discredited. The full humanness of Jesus, on the other hand, is the truest of signs.

Readings

Bowman, David J., S.J., *The Word Made Flesh* (Englewood Cliffs, N. J.: Prentice-Hall, 1963).

Brown, Raymond, S.S., *Jesus: God and Man* (Milwaukee: Bruce, 1967).

"Commonweal Papers, # 2: Jesus," *Commonweal*, November 24, 1967.

Crossan, Dominic, O.S.M., *The Gospel of Eternal Life: Reflections on the Theology of St. John* (Milwaukee: Bruce, 1967).

De Rosa, Peter, *Christ and Original Sin* (Milwaukee: Bruce, 1967).

Jansen, B. M. A., O.P., *An Existential Approach to Theology* (Milwaukee: Bruce, 1966).

Who Is Jesus of Nazareth?, Concilium No. 11 (New York: Paulist Press, 1966).

TRINITY

Modern religious psychology has made the point that as one understands God so fares one's religious life. A person's religious life, in turn, deeply affects his overall psychology. A correct concept of God, therefore, is an extremely important psychological desirable.

Theology has hardly had to wait for modern psychology to know this. The history of theology verifies that the entire life of the Church is to a great extent set by the theology of God that prevails in any given period of Church history. As with grace, one need but check the western and eastern traditions on the theology of the Blessed Trinity to know that the understanding of God has varied in the Church, with considerable practical consequences.

Recent theology has been almost exclusively devoted to the western tradition on the Trinity. In this tradition the Unity of God has been emphasized, with rather sad results for a lively sense of God's true personal life. The personal life of God became the "greatest of the mysteries," left unattended except by the most speculative thinkers. The divine nature and the divine activity received most of the attention, and except for Jesus the personal side of God was known and addressed simply as "God." In the East, on the other hand, Father, Son, and Spirit together were absorbing interests.

Contemporary theology aims mainly at correcting the imbalance in western theology. Concentrating on biblical "personalism" regarding God, and drawing inspiration from eastern thinkers, modern theology endeavors to bring the personal life of God into clearer and more distinctly Christian focus. Its major contribution, having rich implications for practical Christian living, is a scholarly suggestion that Christians enjoy a distinct relationship with each of the divine Persons.

Historical Developments

When Jesus spoke of the Blessed Trinity, when he named God as Father, Son and Spirit, he was careful to insure that his words would be as acceptable to his hearers as possible. He set his teaching, for example, clearly in the framework of what the biblical tradition had already established. He spoke first of the Father, the "Fatherhood" of God being a recognized theological theme in Israel. In identifying himself as Son he acknowledged the primacy of his Father, a point that would have made a great difference to such of his hearers as could at all accept the idea of God's existing as multiple in Person. And his descriptions of the Spirit harmonized uniquely with an historically developed understanding of God's presence, activity, and gifts familiar to Old Testament readers.

Chiefly, though, Jesus took pains that his teaching on Father, Son, and Spirit followed upon an acceptance and trust of himself. His most detailed remarks on the inner, personal life of God were given, for example, only at the Last Supper, and only to the twelve. He had sought to make himself their absorbing preoccupation for three years, and it was upon their acceptance of himself that he based his further disclosure of his own and God's personal mystery. Similarly, in his periodic public references to his own identity in relation to the Father, he endeavored to rest his case on his hearers' acceptance and trust of himself.

It was, therefore, their preoccupation with Jesus that tended as much as anything to keep the apostles and early Christians from "worrying" about the trinity of Persons in God. Jesus had taught that God is Father, Son, and Spirit; and that was sufficient. Doubtless they adjusted their Jewish theology of God to this teaching, as the New Testament clearly shows. But their attention was on Jesus, and their belief in and understanding of Father, Son, and Spirit centered entirely on their belief and trust in him.

Within a hundred and fifty years of the Last Supper, however, the Blessed Trinity had become a central problem for the Church. Many Greek converts were unable to harmonize their Greek notion of God with the Christian belief in Father, Son, and Spirit. Their problem was that of the *equality* of the Three; the Son, they thought, had to be a lesser being than the Father, and so too the Spirit in relation to the Son. Neither could they see how the Son could have taken on real humanity, man's fleshly condition. Their difficulty was understanding Christ's divinity, and to help them the Church's thinkers had to explain the relationship of Jesus as Son of God with the Father and Holy Spirit.

The fruit of their thought was the first installment of the ideas and words that would become classical in the theology of the Trinity. "Equality" was studied, and the notions of "eternal generation" and being "without origin" were developed. There remained, though, no clear ideas on "person" and "nature," and such words as were used served frequently to increase rather than reduce the problem.

By the fourth century the problem had become acute, both in East and West. The *Arians*, against whom the Council of Nicaea sat in A.D. 325, could not admit that Jesus as Son of God was equal in divinity with the Father. They could admit with the mainstream Christians that there was only one God, but they could not accept his activity toward men — the sending of the Son, the redeeming of men, and the work of sanctifying — as manifestations of a threefold and equal personal life in God.

Nor could the mainstream Christians explain themselves very clearly. What they emphasized, though, has meaning even today; namely, that Father, Son, and Spirit reveal(ed) themselves in acts for the sake of men. And though this emphasis on separate acts — sending, redeeming, and sanctifying — ran the danger of a three-Gods theory, the mainstream Christians clung to the notion that by studying these acts one gets some true idea of God's threefold personal life.

This was mainly in the East. In the West the problem led to a development of further ideas and terms. "Oneness in substance and plurality in manifestation" appeared as a lead idea. The word "person" emerged, but hardly in a really helpful sense. At the time it meant "mask," suggesting that in his different acts God manifested merely a different "face." By the time western and eastern thinkers sat down at Nicaea, therefore, emphasis in the West was placed on God's oneness in substance and difference in activity.

As things turned out, though, Nicaea only made matters worse. Western words won out as far as the Creed was concerned, but "substance" and "person" meant exactly the opposite in East and West. To be "one in substance" and "three in person" added up in the East to three individualities equally possessing divinity: in a word, three Gods. While nipping Arianism in the bud, as it were, Nicaea served to split mainstream Christians.

It required another council, that of Constantinople, in A.D. 381, to resolve the issue, which was almost entirely a matter of agreeing on the meaning of words. Providentially, by this time St. Hilary of the West and St. Athanasius of the East had, by reason of forced exile, traveled widely. Leading thinkers of the day, they were able to influence a happy compromise. What emerged was a unanimous acceptance of the "consubstantiality" (oneness in divinity) of Father, Son, and Spirit, and their individual distinctness as Persons holding in common but differently the one divine nature. "One Nature in three Persons" (preferred in the West) or "three Persons in one Nature" (preferred in the East) thus became the classical formula for expressing the mystery of God the Father, God the Son, and God the Holy Spirit.

As with so many other points of theology, it remained for the medieval theologians to complete the work of precision. At their hands the notions of "nature" and "person" received unmistakable clarity and distinction. The divine Nature became the "source of divine activity" and the divine Persons became the "distinct but related personal centers" in which the one divine Nature is equally possessed.

These precisions, however, were unable of themselves to alter the western emphasis on the divine Nature. Here, as elsewhere, the thought of St. Augustine prevailed, who because he had been forced to correct a mistaken notion of God's creative activity, had set the Western Church on a path of attentiveness to God's actions springing from only one source of divine power. And for all that he contributed more than anyone to an understanding of the relationships between Father, Son, and Spirit, his reflections on the unity of their activity in virtue of their one divine Nature carried the greater and lasting impact. Moreover, after the Eastern Schism, generally dated as beginning in A.D. 1054, eastern thought was more and more ignored, and not only because the eastern languages were widely unknown.

Thus, the western tradition never really promoted a personal and inspiring Christian life centering on a familiar knowledge of Father, Son, and Spirit. In the West it was "God" who was always "front and center," as it were, Father, Son, and Spirit being rather vague and intellectually troublesome "background" features of "God." And it became commonplace to assume that clarifying this vagueness was really not very important since, as the main theological notion explained, the separate acts of God toward men — sending, redeeming, and sanctifying — though "attributed" to the individual Persons, are always in fact accomplished by all Three together because of their one divine Nature.

A Different Emphasis Emerges

Modern theologians look upon this theory of appropriation, this "attributing" of special effects to Father, Son, and Spirit, as a kind of prayerful game-playing, a kind of "now you see him now you don't" affair. At least they rather commonly do not *want* to acknowledge that this theory is the last word that can be said on the matter of how Father, Son, and Spirit act and are known. And they have some very solid grounds for this desire.

As early as the seventeenth century a traditional theologian named Petavius raised the question of the Holy Spirit's special relationship to the sanctified Christian. With the tradition he granted that sanctification was an act of "God," but he also insisted that, somewhat in the way the Son alone gives being to Jesus, the Spirit does something alone in the act of sanctifying Christians. It is the *Spirit's* mystery that we share in a particular way when in grace, Petavius insisted.

As variations on this same theme, the thought of Matthias Scheeben, Thomas De Regnon, Emile Mersch, Karl Rahner, and others has successively appeared spanning the nineteenth and twentieth centuries. Their thesis is, in one form or another, that where "God" acts, Father, Son, and Spirit act, and each in their distinctiveness. There is, consequently, something in every divine activity that is special to each of the Persons, and this special thing carries over into what that activity produces.

In everything that God does, therefore, we should be able to detect corresponding signs of Father, Son, and Spirit; and in everything done there is left a basis for seeing it dependent on the Father, on the Son, and on the Spirit, in a word, on each in a distinct and special way. This implies that in every divine activity toward men not only is the divine Nature revealed, but each of the divine Persons; and men, for their part, can understand themselves related not merely to God, but separately and specially — though together — to Father, Son, and Spirit. The implications in all this for "personalizing" Christian spirituality is indeed gratifying, and for pastoral considerations modern theologians are of a mind to pursue rather than relinquish this approach.

Practical Implications

Actually, this more personal approach to the understanding of the Blessed Trinity corresponds clearly with the practical realism of the New Testament and the teaching of many early eastern fathers. It does not, it is true, meet as yet all the demands of logic raised by the western tradition; it remains, in other words, a theory. Yet the simple realism of the sources supporting it can no longer be neglected except at the expense of continuing the ponderous intellectualism and rather sterile spirituality associated with the western tradition.

The chief personal implication of this theory is that Christians meet, know, and relate to each of the divine Persons in a distinct way in every act of God toward them. Everything is *from* the Father, brought about *through* the Son, and implies sharing *in* the Spirit. To each of the Persons Christians can address themselves in praise and gratitude, paying to each a debt separately and personally due. Relating to God can hence be more realistic: Christians can know precisely "Who" rather than "What" it is they are dealing with.

A second and closely related implication is that having special relationships with the Persons of the Trinity provides Christians with a distinct spiritual framework within which to live their lives. Related to the Father, they have a sense of origin and destiny; related to the Son, they have a sense of purpose and work to be done; related to the Spirit, they have a sense of belonging, of sharing, of being loved. No one need look far to see the significance of these and similar awarenesses for personal stabilizing and maturing.

A third implication, one more social than individual, is that the interpersonal or "community" life within God becomes a more prominent backdrop to all Christian endeavors. Too long has

God's "plan" or God's "will" been the standard of what is right and good, an emphasis stemming from an awareness only of God's oneness, of God's Nature. The real standard ultimately is the love-life, the community-life of the divine Persons. Imitating the divine Persons in their total communion with each other is the fundamental law of God for whose fulfillment all other law is designed or to be designed. How pregnant with meaning this is for personal relationships, for family living, even for relations between nations — "This, then, is what I pray, kneeling before the Father, from whom every family, whether spiritual or natural, takes its name" (Eph. 3, 14–15).

Readings

Henry, A., *The Holy Spirit* (New York: Hawthorn Books, 1960), *20th Century Encyclopedia of Catholicism*, Vol. 18.

Salet, Gaston, S.J., "The Trinity: Mystery of Love," in *The Idea of Catholicism*, ed. by W. Burghardt and W. Lynch (New York: Meridian Books, 1960).

Sloyan, Gerard S., *The Three Persons in One God* (Englewood Cliffs: N. J.: Prentice-Hall, 1963).

Spicq, Ceslas, *The Trinity and Our Moral Life According to St. Paul* (Westminster, Md.: Newman, 1963).

Thils, Gustave, *Christian Holiness* (Belgium: Lannoo, 1963), 2nd ed., Part 2, Chap. 1–3.

CHURCH

When you hear the word "Church" you should think the word "mystery." Too long has the word Church been allowed to conjure up what are really inadequate notions both of the meaning and structure of Christ's community.

In an admirable article written shortly before Vatican II, the late Gustave Weigel, S.J., traced the history of this word. His study is uniquely helpful toward understanding contemporary thought on the Church.

Shifting Images

Scripture, Father Weigel noted, piles up some forty images as descriptions of the Church. Kingdom, Bride, Temple, Body, Net, Flock, Banquet, and People are perhaps the most familiar of these. Each of these images portrays some side of the Church. The entire collection is required, however, to give anything like an adequate picture of the Church's many-sided reality, and a neglect of any of them breeds a distorted view of the Church.

In each era of the Church's long history, nonetheless, one or other of these images has been preferred over the others. Some feature of the Church has been more evident, more appealing, or more readily understood than others, and thus its biblical image has become especially popular.

In recent centuries the preferred image was that of Kingdom. European nationalism, featuring as it did all the trappings of political kingdoms, made the notion of Kingdom easily understandable. The sad aspect of this, according to Weigel, was that the Kingdom image with which bishops, theologians, and laity identified the Church was not that of the Kingdom of God portrayed in the Scriptures. Rather, it was the kingdom notion prevalent in the political structures of sixteenth-, seventeenth-, and eighteenth-century Europe.

In the nineteenth century the idea of Society came to the fore, a process furthered by the emergence of both democracy and communism. Most adults today remember the emphasis their catechisms gave to understanding the Church as the "Society instituted by Christ." The point stressed was the Church's oneness of purpose, power of authority, and capability of fulfilling its goal, all of which were essential ingredients of a society as defined by classical thinkers.

Throughout these centuries the burden of attention was placed on external features of the Church, especially on its authority structure. This was done to support the Roman Catholic Church's claims against Protestants on the one hand, and the whole Christian community's claims against the unjust pressures of European States on the other.

In recent decades attention has gradually shifted from the external structure of the Church to its inner and invisible nature. The first sign of this, according to Weigel, was Karl Adam's pioneering study called, in translation from the German, *The Spirit of Catholicism*. This was followed some years later by Emile Mersch's monumental French work entitled *The Whole Christ*. Pius XII's encyclical *On the Mystical Body* came, in 1943, as a high point in this trend.

Of a sudden the Catholic community found itself in possession of an understanding of the Church considerably richer than that found in its regular textbooks. But this situation was not experienced without controversy and suffering. Some of the most respected writers of the day had to recast the fruit of long years of study. Teachers had to revise their lecture notes. Sermons changed. Overnight, as it were, the Church had become the *Mystical Body of Christ* rather than the *Society instituted by Christ*. And few really knew what it was all about.

An Image For Today

For twenty years, between 1940 and 1960, the faithful were regularly instructed in the meaning of the Mystical Body image. As often as not the instruction was more academic than inspiring, but by the time of Vatican II, which Father Weigel's survey does not include, familiarity with that image was widespread. For all practical purposes it had become the most serviceable key to an understanding of the Church.

Then came the surprising insinuations of the *Constitution on the Church* published by the Council in 1964. The bishops had found even the Mystical Body image lacking as a principal description of the Church at this time. Far more adequate, they implied, is the People of God image. Once again the burden of rethinking the Church fell upon teachers, priests, and laity.

What advantages does the People of God image have over previously preferred images? This question has to be answered in light of what men of today are concerned about. It also has to be answered in light of the better understanding of Scripture that is a feature of the present time. Always to be remembered, though, is that no single image can ever carry the whole "mystery" of the Church, and little is ever gained by an overemphasis of one image to the neglect of others.

The Mystical Body image emphasized the mystery of Christ's union with all the members of the Church. It had the advantage of stressing the spiritual side of the Church's mystery over its external, political side. Its disadvantage was an inherent inability to bring into prominence the communal, historical, and collegial features of the Church.

The People of God image is able to do all that the Mystical Body image did, and more. It focuses attention on the Church as a community, a nation, possessed of a common identity and spirit, a common bond of unity. It portrays that community as a historically evolving reality, struggling against sin and time toward the fullest achievement of its unique "manifest destiny." And it conveys the idea of the Church as a community for whose weal and woe all its members are responsible, and to whose progress all must contribute.

Continuing development

Though there is a remarkable harmony between the People of God image and the mood of modern man, it would be quite wrong to suppose that that image stands for a definitive and final understanding of the Church. The shifting of understanding that preceded the Council is just as apparent in developments since the Council. In fact, the People of God image, with all the richness of understanding it conjures up, may be even more short-lived than the Mystical Body image in terms of relevance to the times.

What has to be faced, for example, is that the People of God image is ultimately an Old Testament notion. It lends itself to being enriched by New Testament insights, and can easily "carry" such understanding as the Christian community has developed about itself. St. Peter's first letter (2:9–10) clearly bears this out.

But there is a problem in this. The Church is the Christian community, and whether the People of God image does full justice to the "community in Christ" idea of the Church is a good question. And today the same question arises with respect to the "ecumenical" and even "secular" aspects of the Church. The Church as "mystery," after all, to say nothing of some of its features as "institution," is to be found not only in separated Christian communities and non-Christian religious communities, but even in the world at large.

Surely one can read into the People of God image all these ideas. But one can do this with the Mystical Body image and many of the other biblical images as well. Nor is it required that one image be expected to carry the whole reality of the Church adequately; this would be impossible. What is advantageous, however, is to find one image which at this particular time *best* conveys that understanding of the Church which *best* fits the times.

As the days pass since the Council and the fruit of reflecting on the Council's teaching takes clearer form, it seems that the community and ecumenical aspects of the Church are coming ever more into prominence. And not far behind is the secular aspect of the Church, the realization that Christ forms persons in his Spirit through nature and world events even independently of the services of the Church. The prominence of these aspects of the Church may well lead to a replacing of the People of God image with another image, even a nonbiblical one.

The New Testament writers themselves struggled to "describe" the Church with images richer than those found in the Old Testament. Theologians may soon find themselves in much the same position with respect even to the New Testament. The "family" image, for example, one that was frequently appealed to in speeches at the Council and given prominence in the American Bishops' pastoral on *The Church in Our Day*, is not unconditionally a biblical image; neither is it without its drawbacks for the present day. To suggest, therefore, that the Church may soon be best described for contemporary man simply as the *Christian community*, or the *Community of Persons in Christ*, seems not at all an unorthodox novelty.

The Christian Community

The Church is a community ultimately because it is a sign of Christ, of his being for "the many." What better way could Christ's being "for all" be portrayed in a human manner than in a community? This is the same question on a broader scale that can be asked of his Incarnation: what better way could God's personal love for men be manifested than by the loving kindness of a Man giving himself for others even to the point of complete Self-sacrifice? The answer is that there could be no better way.

The Church is a community, too, because it is a sign of Christ's fullness of saving power. Portraying this fullness in a human way is best done by parceling out this fullness among many, by giving it to be shared in different ways and degrees. Christ is Prophet, Priest, and King: he alone calls with the word of God, gives life for fellowship with God, subdues in loving commitment to God. So the Church is empowered for teaching, sanctifying, and governing, possessing within itself the fullness of Christ's Word, Priesthood, and Authority, but as distributed in different degrees among its members in order the better to give this fullness human manifestation.

The Church, therefore, is a community manifesting Christ's uniqueness, his being the sole Savior of men. For this reason there is only one saving community, one Church. And the Church manifests Christ's fullness or universality of saving power, his being Savior for "the many." For this reason the Church is a *structured, hierarchic* community, having ranks and degrees.

It pertains to the Church's being a community-sign of Christ that it has bishops, priests, deacons, and laity. Only by this variation of rank is the fullness of Christ adequately portrayed in a human way. All the ranks together, that is, the community as a whole, portray the complete fullness of Christ. Each of the ranks taken singly portrays this fullness to a certain degree; each of the ranks manifests Christ as Prophet, Priest, and King. But each higher rank focuses this fullness, as it were, more clearly and unmistakably. Each rank, moreover, brings to light, makes more clear, some feature of that fullness in a particular way: bishops disclose Christ as Prophet or Teacher; priests and deacons disclose Christ as Priest, offering gifts to God and distributing his gifts to men; laity disclose Christ as King, subduing all things to God's saving reign.

And to the structure of the Church is added Christ's mission and power. The Church is a community-sign not only of Christ's past coming and heavenly achievement, but of his continuing presence and activity. Christ came, sent by the Father, not to leave, but to abide with men always, to be the one Savior present and active among men until the end of time. The Church, therefore, is a community-sign that is also a sacrament. It "contains" what it signifies, and is empowered to bring that about in every era of human history.

The mission of Christ is embodied in the Church. The Church, thus, is to call, sanctify, and subdue all men with respect to the reign of God. The power of the Church, like that of Christ, is the Gospel (the Word), the power of priesthood (sacred orders), and sacramental character(s). Both the threefold mission of Christ and threefold power of Christ rest upon and permeate all ranks in the Church, but again in different degrees of intensity. Each rank is sent and empowered as a "sacrament" of Christ, each is responsible and equipped for the total work of Christ, but each in a different way and to a different degree. It is the entire Church, with all its ranks, that bears the fullness of Christ's mission and power, that is, the "sacrament" of the fullness of Christ's presence and activity for all days.

And as a community of men, as was the case with Christ himself, the Church is historical. It grows, as Christ himself grew. It is in process toward glory: Christ's Spirit only gradually unfolds within the community and takes expression through it.

Christ, too, by the fact of incarnation, was at a "distance" from the Father; his life was steadily a "going to the Father."

With the Church the "distance" is not solely of human and spirit growth, as was the case with Christ. With the Church it is also a matter of winning release from sinfulness. Only gradually is the Church an ever "fuller" sign of Christ, but in her case it is not only a matter of deepening faith, hope, and charity in the manner of Christ's growth, nor simply of becoming more of a community of persons maturing according to the process of personalism, but of a continuing purifying of herself through repentance and renewal from sins and the effects of sin. And only to the extent that the whole Church gives itself to this threefold process of growth, only to the extent that the Church becomes an ever deeper and fuller community of grace, personalism, and sinlessness, will the presence and power of Christ be evident in and through her.

Readings

Abbott & Gallagher (eds.), *Constitution on the Church*, in *The Documents of Vatican II* (New York: Guild Press, 1966).

The Church in Our Day, American Bishops' Pastoral (Washington, D. C.: U. S. Catholic Conference, 1968).

Smith, Hilary, O.C.D., "The Family Fallacy," in *Review For Religious*, November, 1966, pp. 1000–1018.

Weigel, Gustave, S.J., "Catholic Ecclesiology in Our Time," in *Christianity Divided*, edited by Callahan (New York, Sheed & Ward, 1961).

PART FOUR

Sacramental Problems

RITUAL

Much has been written on the theology of sacraments in our day; not nearly enough has been written, however, on sacramental ritual. To be sure, Vatican Council II called for a re-doing of sacramental rites. And this call had as a setting decades of historical and theological scholarship. Moreover, practical alterations have already been made in the celebrating of most sacraments, especially the Eucharist. Vernacular languages are common, modern music for worship is appearing, responsible experimentation is being allowed. Surely the mood and practice with respect to sacramental rites is different today than it was in recent times.

Whether this really means something "new" has been brought forth or merely that we are placing a "patch on an old garment" is a good question. And whether one can really speak of a difference of response to this question on the part of recent and contemporary theology is something else again. There are threads of thought dangling around today, however, which, gathered together, represent at least one side of contemporary theology's approach to the matter of sacramental ritual.

Historical Considerations

At the heart of ritual developments in the early Church was the need and practice of the local Churches. During the era of the Church Fathers, from the apostles to the sixth century, the main structure of sacramental ritual that we know today was worked out. This was done, surely, with an eye to what other Christian communities were doing, but it was also done, and principally, with a view to the practical participation and instruction of the local community. Many of the Fathers themselves developed "rites" for their own people, and others gave approval to those worked out by their collaborators. That this was mainly accomplished with a view to local needs is illustrated by the surprisingly large variety of rites that existed at that time and which still continue to adorn the Church today.

In this process of development there is no doubt that the Roman Church held an exemplary primacy. How they *did* things in Rome was in many ways as influential as how they *believed* things in Rome. Here was a community rightly celebrated for its apostolic origin, its excellence in charity, and its purity of doctrine. Its doctrinal influence was one thing, however, and its ritual influence another. Whereas there was little or no contest with respect to following its lead in faith, there was a tempered reserve with respect to endorsing all its ritual practices. In the earliest centuries, in fact, other communities served as even more popular patterns of ritual than did that of Rome.

As time went on the shifting political and social situation in the West gave the Roman Church a greater prestige among the Churches than it had previously enjoyed, and with this prestige came power. Through a gradual and highly complex process, involving as much the free decisions of local communities as the missionary and reform tactics of the Roman Church and Empire, there emerged for the Roman Church an authoritative primacy in ritual as well as doctrine. This is not to say that the Roman rite became the sole sacramental ritual in the Church. Both East and West continued to exhibit ritual variations, due at times only to a calculated defense of their traditions. But more and more Churches in the West did come under the influence of the Roman rite, and the Roman Church itself worked both to bring this about and to maintain it.

During the expanse of centuries called the Middle Ages the Roman rite definitely became the "norm" in most Churches in the West. Fidelity to it became a legal matter, and both its meaning and "universality" were given theological explanation. It was regarded as a sign of the Church's unity and catholicity, and of its mission and capacity to bring the Word and Food of Life to God's Kingdom on earth without error or defect.

What went generally unobserved in all this was the continuing shifting of the political and social scene, a shifting that had deep psychological and spiritual impact on the population of the West. Languages changed, thought-patterns altered, life-styles varied. And in the wake of this shifting the pastoral needs of local communities grew accordingly.

That all this went effectively unobserved is demonstrated by the Reformation. What began then as a pastoral effort, what at least had a vivid pastoral ring about it, became in due time a doctrinal conflict. Distracted by doctrinal problems, the Council of Trent, too, left unattended the needed pastoral renewal of the Church.

To be sure, that Council legislated any number of key reforms. Always, though, as far as ritual was concerned, these envisioned greater fidelity to the Roman rite. And the "established" ritual became even more entrenched as the decades passed, due to the emphasis on ecclesiastical tradition and authority that came to typify the Catholic Church's reaction to Protestantism.

From the sixteenth to the nineteenth century theologians concentrated on "explaining" the Church's *magisterium*, that is, her teaching mission and authority. Her legislative mission was also examined, and in light of the conclusions that were drawn the "theological" value of the Roman rite took on special significance.

During the nineteenth century, and extending into our own day, this "magisterial" emphasis reached its height. At this time it became commonplace among theologians to illustrate the "ordinary infallibility" of the Church by pointing to the universal laws of the Church. These, it was said, cannot be detrimental to the salvation of the faithful because of the presence and unerring protective influence of Christ in the Church. Under this heading came the rituals of the Roman Rite, which were regarded at this time with much the same spirit as was accorded the universal doctrine of the Church.

There was a problem inherent in this, and even the best of recent theologians bear witness to a discussion regarding the "obligatory" nature of sacramental rites. Authors like Noldin, Merkelbach, Prummer, and Cappello commonly spoke of an attempt to distinguish rites into those that are *preceptive* and those that are merely *directive*. To the former class were assigned such rites as look to the validity of sacraments, for example, and such as could not be omitted without likelihood of "scandal." The latter, on the other hand, were such rites as are only loosely connected with sacramental celebration, and for that reason are to be considered "guidelines" for ordinary situations but not necessarily "obligations" in every situation. And the authors in question did not wholly reject the truth of this distinction, though for the sake of uniformity with respect to observing the Roman rite they were consistently reserved in justifying its practical application.

Some Observations on the Past

The history of Christian ritual indicates several significant facts. One is that in the earliest centuries local Churches, under the guidance of their bishops, designed their own rites to suit their own needs. To be sure, this was not a process undertaken in complete independence of neighboring Churches, and in this regard the Roman Church enjoyed a certain primacy. But the right of self-determination in matters of ritual was jealously guarded by most of the ancient Churches, and some of this spirit has remained alive in particular areas of the Church, both in East and West, even to the present day.

Another fact is that originally faith and theology inspired ritual rather than the other way around. With the expanding of the Roman rite throughout the West, ritual itself became an inspiration of faith and theology. It became a commonplace in the Western Church, in other words, to think and teach that because things were done in a certain way there were solid reasons for believing in a certain way. Though correct to a certain extent, this attitude led to a forgetting that what originally inspired even the Roman rite was, rather, the understanding that because things are believed and understood in a certain way it is fitting that things be done in a certain way.

A third fact is that the equating of doctrine and ritual in importance is a tendency that has always been resisted by some, even during the nineteenth and early twentieth centuries' "golden age" of "magisterial" theology. Even the most reputable writers of the period acknowledged the general validity of distinguishing essentials from accidentals with respect to ritual, and expressed at least a general willingness to assign a corresponding proportionate authority or value to each.

Contemporary Realizations

If we join to these observations drawn from history certain realizations widespread in the Church today, the place and authority of ritual in the Church becomes even clearer. Chief among these realizations is that noted even in Vatican II's *Constitution on the Liturgy;* namely, that the cultural differences among peoples not only justify but require ritual variations corresponding to these differences. In principle, in other words, it is realized that ritual is at least in part a matter of local design. The *Constitution* applies this principle in terms of national regions and local dioceses, and, properly understood, this is sufficient. Implied, though, is the inherent extension of this principle also to parishes and analogous congregations, like convents, campuses, etc.

And as for cultural differences, the *Constitution,* being a pastoral document and concerned with the usual and ordinary things, does not stress that only those differences have worth that are deeply rooted and verified by high scholarship. As sacramental signs are always evaluated "according to the common estimation of men," so cultural differences are to be taken according to their obvious rather than congenital existence. Subsequent commentary on the *Constitution,* both authoritative and reputable, makes this unmistakable. That American *youth* take to guitar Masses, for example, is a genuine cultural difference, even though guitar playing and the melodies they identify with are not clearly traceable, say, to the days of Stephen Foster and through every decade afterward.

Another realization abroad today is that ritual expresses the Church's faith and has theological value on this basis only. One cannot write a theology on the basis of ritual, since ritual is of human rather than revealed origin. Furthermore, insofar as ritual embodies a celebrating and responding to realities believed in, it is a matter of surveillance on the part of the whole Church, that is, on the part of those responsible for the belief and practice of the whole Church. To the extent that orthodoxy of belief and suitability of celebration are insured, however, ritual is a matter both of design and surveillance for the local Church or congregation.

Ritual, moreover, like the mission of the Church of which it is a part, has a twofold objective: communicating the faith of the Church and drawing the faithful as deeply as possible into the realities with which the faith is concerned. Celebrating the sharing in those realities, that is, ritual, must aim at fulfilling both these objectives. It must portray in sign what is truly believed by the Church, and, of equal importance, it must draw the faithful into an ever deeper sharing in those realities.

Not all rites and rubrics have the same value toward achieving these objectives, nor is the Church equally guarded by Christ in fulfilling both sides of her mission. She always retains the fullness of Christ's doctrine, for all that she may not understand or proclaim that wholeness adequately. But this is not to say that she always so proclaims or celebrates the realities "behind" that doctrine as to bring about the fullest possible participation in them.

To be sure, it can be said, and the faithful must in fact agree, that the universal laws of the Church, including ritual, will not lead to perdition. The presence and assistance of Christ protects the Church from so governing as to lead Christians away from Christ. But it may be seriously doubted whether Church laws, universal or not, always lead to the fullness of participation in Christ. The very phenomenon of renewal argues against this. In the case of ritual, it may be held, and perhaps should be so held especially by those responsible for the pastoral welfare of the faithful, that rubrics and rites can even work against the fuller engaging of the faithful in the mysteries ritually celebrated.

Conclusions

The Roman rite, as any other rite, therefore, has theological and pastoral validity only to the degree that it adequately discharges the twofold mission of the Church. Since there are many ways of ritually portraying and celebrating the fullness of the Church's faith, any rite, insofar as it does this, is as good as another. The primacy of one over another is mainly a matter of cultural taste and pastoral effectiveness. In the order of practice, moreover, tradition, no matter how ancient, no matter even if of apostolic origin, has nothing of value comparable to anything pertaining to the order of belief or doctrine. The two orders are quite distinct, and they should never be allowed to be confused in our thinking.

Second, in any rite that is duly authorized as a practical embodiment of genuine belief and suitable celebration, a distinction must always be retained and pastorally followed between what deals with proclaiming the faith and what deals with drawing the congregation more deeply into that faith. In practical terms this means that the celebrating of ritual must always have a due element of congregation-centeredness. It must allow generously for such on-the-spot variation as looks directly to making it pastorally effective.

Orthodoxy is not the only thing with which ritual deals. Pastoral effectiveness is equally important. And this latter is as much the responsibility of the celebrating minister as of those under whose authority he celebrates. It is, moreover, as much the business of the congregation as it is of the celebrating minister. Ritual, therefore, must always be a "collaborated" enterprise in the Church; otherwise it has no practical Christian purpose.

Readings

Häring, Bernard, C.Ss.R., *The Law of Christ* (Westminster, Md.: Newman, 1963), Vol. 2, Chaps. 5–6.

——— *A Sacramental Spirituality* (New York: Sheed & Ward, 1962).

Jungmann, Josef A., S.J., *Public Worship — A Survey* (Collegeville, Minn.: Liturgical Press, 1957), esp. Chap. 2: "History."

O'Meara, Thomas F., O.P., "Liturgy Hot and Cool," *Worship*, April, 1968, pp. 215–222.

Schillebeeckx, Edward, O.P., *Christ the Sacrament of the Encounter With God* (New York: Sheed & Ward, 1963), esp. pp. 100 ff.

Wolf, Donald J., S.J., and Schall, James V., S.J., *Current Trends in Theology* (New York: Doubleday, 1965), Chap. 5: "Contemporary Liturgical Revival."

PENANCE

There is a problem with the sacrament of penance today, but it is not so much between "old" and "new" theology as between established and recommended practice. Secret, oft-repeated devotional confession is, of course, based on a definite theology. This theology, however, is not so definite as to be at odds with contemporary thought on the matter. Fundamentally, recent and contemporary theology on confession are the same. Contemporary theology merely adds insights that would support a change of practice. That a change of practice is needed, however, is based on something else, namely, a growing disenchantment with private devotional confession.

The Problem

Countless people throughout the Church are asking: what meaning does frequent and private devotional confession have for Christians living today?

To this question, frankly, there is no ready answer. Theologians have only begun to treat it; Vatican II did not even consider it. It is still too soon to expect a full answer. Many in fact do not as yet even see the problem prompting the question. Before long, however, confession is going to be one of the very pressing pastoral problems of the Church. If it is not, there will be good reason to doubt the depth of the renewal initiated by Vatican II.

The most obvious reason why confession is becoming a problem for many is their deepening awareness of the Eucharist as *the* sacrament of Christian growth. The root of the difficulty is the Eucharist's own inner capacity to forgive sin.

The faith of the Church in this aspect of the Eucharist is ancient. The Council of Trent was merely summing up centuries of tradition when it spoke of the Eucharist as "an anti-dote by which we can be freed from daily faults and preserved from mortal sin." In 1905, in his decree re-establishing the practice of daily communion, St. Pius X expressed the same belief: daily communion is desirable "for cleansing away the light faults which daily occur, and for avoiding the graver sins to which human frailty is prone."

With the widespread practice of daily and weekly communion in the Church, it is hardly to be wondered that many of the faithful are beginning to see the Eucharist rather than penance as *the* sacrament of "regular" or "routine" forgiveness. That many, by the same token, are becoming confused as to the exact meaning of devotional confession is also not surprising.

It is true, of course, that as recently as 1943, in Pius XII's encyclical *On the Mystical Body of Christ,* the Church made a strong statement on the value of devotional confession. The relationship between this practice and frequent communion was not explained, however; it was not even mentioned. And that was twenty-five years ago. As things move today, it seems proper to suggest that now the Church may be looking at the matter somewhat differently. At issue, though, is not so much the value of devotional confession as the manner of its practice. This is clear from another aspect of the growing problem.

Contemporary theology is especially sensitive to the social side of sin. Modern theologians constantly repeat this theme, which is beginning to "rub off" on more and more of the faithful. All sin leaves people in some way unable to answer fully to the call or needs of Christ in his Church. To sin is to let the Church down.

The forgiveness of sin, then, necessarily implies a reshaping of relationship with the Church. Some theologians are inclined to see this implication as the first effect of the sacrament of penance. This effect differs, of course, in the case of mortal and venial sin, but in either case it is first a reshaping of relationship with the Church, and then with God.

As this idea becomes more familiar the inadequacies of present confessional procedures will become more glaring. There is little or nothing in a ritual of calculated isolation, darkness, and whispering that illustrates in sacramental sign the social side either of sin or forgiveness. Since sacraments are to make theological realities as explicit as possible, something has to be done regarding penance.

A Possible Solution

Until the liturgy of penance receives as much attention as that of the Eucharist it is going to become more and more difficult to "sell" devotional confession to the knowledgeable faithful. What can be done? Taking a number of well-established traditional points of doctrine and practice a bit more seriously would go a long way toward a solution.

First to be recalled is the fact that venial sins, previously confessed mortal sins, and imperfections never impose an obligation of confession. These comprise the "free" matter of devotional confessions. Not even the law of annual confession binds a person who has nothing to confess but "free" matter.

Second, confessors have always been allowed, and at times even required, to give absolution when a complete statement of sins is impossible or inadvisable. No priest is to refuse absolution to one acknowledging general sinfulness without a statement of specific sins, when it is obvious that the sinfulness in question deals with "free" matter. Though not an ordinary procedure, the point is that for a good reason a priest can settle for a mere sign of general sorrow for sinfulness when granting absolution rather than requiring a specific listing of sins.

Third, general absolution of all sins without confession is regularly given in situations of emergency or great difficulty. The battlefield and disaster scene illustrate this. Sins absolved in this way are truly forgiven, though mortal sins have yet to be told in one's next confession. Even mortal sins, therefore, can for a serious reason be absolved prior to their being confessed.

From the tradition, then, one can gather three important items: venial sins do not have to be confessed; for a good reason some general sign of repented sinfulness can be substituted for a specific listing of sins in the case of "free" matter; and for a serious reason general absolution can be given even to those in mortal sin without previous confession. Solving the growing problem of devotional confession requires that these items be taken *seriously*. What they imply is that devotional confession need not be so much a matter of the confessional "box" as simply of absolution.

To these items contemporary theology adds certain pastoral and liturgical considerations. It also makes some just criticisms of the present practice of devotional confession. These things too are to be taken seriously.

The person-centeredness of contemporary theology lays emphasis not on traditional *examples* of "good" or "serious" reasons for omitting the listing of sins prior to absolution, but on the *principle* that for such reasons absolution can be given without the listing of sins. Emphasis is placed on the needs of the penitent(s), of the Church, not on consistency with past examples. Curing disenchantment toward a sacrament is itself a "good" reason for altering sacramental procedures. Widespread disenchantment is a "serious" reason. The point is that pastoral practice must cure rather than promote problems, and a distaste for the sacraments, especially penance, has always been treated with great liberality by the Church and reputed moralists. It must not be otherwise today.

Contemporary theology also emphasizes the liturgical aspect of penance. All the sacraments are liturgy, and liturgy means mystery, community, and celebration. For all that the present procedure of devotional confession is a genuine version of liturgy, it is a very poor version. It is neither community nor celebration in any way adequate to the mystery it embodies. To correct this, and especially to draw the faithful more deeply into the mystery of penance, is, again, a "good" and even "serious" reason for altering confessional procedures. "The salvation of souls is the supreme law" — whereas the tradition brought this axiom to bear in emergencies, contemporary theology insists that its first meaning is the preventing of emergencies, the curing of situations that are in any way suppressive of genuine spirituality and Christian growth.

Finally, contemporary theology criticizes present confessional practice for furthering a regrettable individualism in Christian piety. Countless penitents indicate an undesirable "Jesus and I" preoccupation; and corrective counseling, especially when limited to the confessional, as is the usual case, seems not of itself a sufficient cure. Many penitents stream regularly to confession, moreover, consciously or unconsciously feeling *obliged* to cleanse themselves of "free" matter by this means. For these, confession is not so much a matter of reshaping a relationship with Christ or the Church as a releasing of themselves from guilt anxieties: they have tarnished their self-image and cannot live with themselves until cleansed by the ritual of sacramental purgation. Not a little harmful both to themselves and the Church, this misconception is, again, hardly reduced by present confessional practice.

Neither is the strain on confessors given any notice. Some in the regular crowd of penitents have needs of a kind deserving priority over the personal "sedatives" sought by the many. Present procedures simply do not allow for this priority in any truly human way, neither on the part of the confessor nor of those "standing in line." The most fruitful administration and reception of the sacrament of penance possible — itself a law — is thus rendered a phantasy.

What all this comes down to is that for the good of persons, for the good of the Church, devotional confession should periodically be celebrated publicly and by way of general absolution. Due instruction should precede and accompany such a "penance festival," and it should be prepared for and celebrated well. But it should be done. The Ember Days would be ideal occasions for this; at least once in Lent and Advent would be appropriate. The penitential character of these days or seasons would thus be reinforced, and the greater needs of the many coming to confession only at Easter and/or Christmas better provided for.

Some theologians and bishops are inclined to resist this solution on doctrinal grounds, seeing as the only alternate to present practice a public "service of preparation" as a framework for private confession. Their reservation is based on the Council of Trent's teaching that all mortal sins must be specifically listed in confession. Since publicly celebrated general absolution would dispense with this they feel that Trent's dogmatic declaration would be thereby voided, a situation that the Church simply cannot sponsor.

It is not at all certain, however, especially in light of the traditional items described earlier, that public general absolution raises a doctrinal problem of any kind. That it raises a problem is undeniable, but of a pastoral not of a doctrinal nature. This problem is twofold: how to insure that those in mortal sin receiving general absolution will fulfill the obligation set forth by the Council of Trent at their next confession, and how to insure that the use of private confession will not become identified with being in mortal sin. These difficulties are surmountable, however: by frequent instruction, and by restricting "public penance" to several times a year without diminishing either the availability or freedom of private confession.

The real nub of the problem is the extending of "good" and "serious" reasons for general absolution to include a sacramental or liturgical enrichment of the faithful. Recent theology, for one reason or another, did not think along this line. Contemporary theology, on the other hand, sets primacy on it. Only when this latter way of thinking prevails will the problem of devotional confession be solved.

Until Then

Whether celebrated publicly or privately the sacrament of penance has its own identity, even in relation to the Eucharist. Concentrating on this will also be of help in making its devotional reception meaningful.

Penance aims at freeing us from ourselves, from those barriers of isolation and self-concern that are the heart of sin. It aims at releasing our religious and moral energies for self-giving and service. Penance opens us; it frees us for love, for love born of faith.

Penance differs from the Eucharist in that the latter sacrament bolsters such love-energies as have already been released from the hold of the "flesh." In "cleansing away the light faults which daily occur" the Eucharist is healing love-tendencies already released but not yet perfectly directed or animated.

The remission of sins in penance, on the other hand, even when these are merely venial, is more that of freeing newer and as yet shackled love-energies. It makes us more free in that it releases more of our basic potential for love from the hold of our fallen nature. The Eucharist draws us outward in self-giving; it attracts and inspires to love. It gives form and "spirit" to such of our love-energies as have already been freed. The specific contribution of penance is the very releasing of those outgoing capacities upon which the attractive force of the Eucharist can directly attend.

Readings

Häring, Bernard, C.Ss.R., *Shalom: Peace: The Sacrament of Reconciliation* (New York: Farrar, Straus, and Giroux, 1967).

Leclercq, Jean, O.S.B., "Confession and Praise of God," *Worship*, March, 1968, pp. 169–176.

McCormick, Richard A., S.J., "Notes on Moral Theology: January-June, 1967," *Theological Studies*, December, 1967, pp. 769–776.

Nolan, Joseph T., "Communion Before Confession — When?" *National Catholic Reporter*, Vol. 4, # 10, January 3, 1967, p. 10.

————— "General Absolution: the need for it, the case for it," *National Catholic Reporter*, Vol. 4, # 13, January 24, 1967, p. 8.

Orsy, Ladislas M., S.J., "The Sacrament of Penance in Religious Communities," *Worship*, March, 1968, pp. 159–168.

EUCHARIST

It is customary for theologians to treat the Eucharist under
three headings: Sacrifice, Sacrament, and Real Presence. They
do this because the Eucharist readily exhibits these three features.
A problem arises, however, when one or other of these features
is given undue primacy over the others, or when the three are
so strictly distinguished as to confuse their relationship. In either
event the unity of the Eucharist stands to be lost.

Recent theology unwittingly made both these mistakes, and
as a consequence the Church has for several centuries suffered
from a severely inadequate grasp of her greatest treasure. Contemporary theology, for its part, has busied itself with rectifying
this: first, by searching out the scriptural teaching on the Eucharist more profoundly, thereby setting the conclusions of recent
theology in a richer and unifying context; and second, by bringing to bear on the Eucharist modern insights into the meaning
of such things as sign, substance, and presence. The result has
been, in the main, to give the Church a fuller and clearer
understanding of the Eucharist than it has perhaps ever possessed.

Liturgy and Real Presence

Because of their great respect for the Eucharist as the re-pre-
sentation of Christ's sacrifice on Calvary, and of Holy Communion as a personal meeting with Christ, theologians of recent
centuries tended to treat the real presence of Christ in the
Eucharist as a "special question" at the end of their discussion.
What resulted from this in the minds of many was a divorcing
of the real presence from the Eucharist as a whole. This, in
turn, served to reinforce an individualistic and sentimental trend
in spirituality whose roots lay in the liturgical ignorance, or one-
sidedness, of the Middle Ages. The Mass was thought important,

and the sacrament of the Eucharist even more so, but what really mattered was that Jesus was truly present — on the altar at Mass, within oneself at communion, in the tabernacle always.

This impulse was not wholly a mistake. Contemporary theology also sets primacy on the real presence. But no longer is it a matter of separating real presence from other features of the Eucharist. Instead, real presence is seen as a key for tying all features of the Eucharist into a fitting unity. Chiefly it is a key for situating the Eucharist in the mystery of the Church.

The Eucharist, according to contemporary theologians, is essentially *liturgy*. This means that it is worship in sign. More specifically, it is God's saving activity joined with man's appreciation and response, both co-existing and co-enacted in symbolic acts. This understanding was at the heart of Old Testament liturgy, and Old Testament liturgy, in turn, was both the inspiration and setting of Christ's instituting of the Eucharist.

Chief among the Old Testament liturgies was that of Passover. In this celebration of sacrificed Passover lamb and sacred meal the saving intervention of God was both commemorated and believed to be made present and renewed. Even apart from the Passover it was believed in Israel, according to Father Louis Bouyer, that a pious reading of the Scriptures made God present and active, and even the ordinary meal, when blessed, was thought a "sacrament" of communion both with God and the persons participating. In the Temple liturgies and the liturgical meals associated with these, this faith reached a climax, as surely was the case with Passover. Real Presence, therefore, was central to the very notion of liturgy in the Old Testament.

Eucharist as Sacrifice

It was precisely into the Passover liturgical context that Jesus placed himself as the Lamb of God to be slain for the saving of God's People — "This is my body *given* for you . . . this is my blood *poured out* for you."

Jesus knew himself as the presence of God. At the Last Supper he gave this presence a new form, a new focusing, a new and unmistakable intensity. Taking all the liturgical meaning of Passover, both its sacrificial and banquet aspects, he gave it fuller meaning: he changed it from prophecy to fulfillment, from suggestion to reality. To the Passover bread and wine he communicated his own priestly being, changing them from signs of promise to signs of his own self-offering in the name of the Father. His priestly being, embodied in the flesh since his birth, Jesus now gave new and further form: Passover-food form. On the morrow he would give it sacrificial-death form, and by means of that, through resurrection, it would achieve glory form. His life, his Eucharist, his death, his glory — all are signs of the one and same self-offering of the Son of God for the sake of men.

It is in this very notion of *presence* that recent and contemporary theology differ the most in understanding the Eucharist as sacrifice. In recent theology the emphasis was on the Eucharist's making present the sacrifice of Calvary. So emphatic did this become that the "mystery" theory of Odo Casel, an early twentieth-century German scholar, led to the understanding that if the Eucharist sign were suddenly to be removed the Mass would portray before our eyes the very agony of Jesus on the Cross.

In contemporary theology emphasis is placed on the self-offering of the Son of God, on his eternal priestly relationship toward the Father translated by the incarnation into human form, and taking ever more clearly focused manifestation: first in Jesus' life, then in the Passover bread and wine, then on the Cross, and finally in his resurrection and glorification.

The two approaches differ in that the one concentrates on Calvary in isolation, as it were, and the other on Calvary within the framework of Jesus' priestly being and continuing sacrificial self-offering in time and eternity. The Eucharist is Calvary, to be sure, according to contemporary theology; but more: it is the Son of God, High-Priest of creation and heaven, whose act on Calvary completed his earthly priesthood and inaugurated his heavenly one. It is Calvary in that it is the One who gave himself totally there in one way and who continues now (and forever) that same total Self-giving in another way. The Eucharist is Calvary in that it is the One produced by Calvary, the One who there gave himself completely in the flesh, and who now lives forever in that act of total offering in the flesh (now glorified) that he achieved at that moment.

The act of Calvary has passed; the Eucharist does not make

present the bleak hillside incident of the crucifixion. What it makes present is the Victim and Priest of Calvary, and the self-same priestly act of Calvary, since on the cross Jesus achieved in the flesh that totality of self-offering in which, by glorification, he is now forever consecrated and sealed. The Eucharist is a symbol of Calvary: the separate consecration of bread and wine, and their eating, symbolize admirably the self-giving of Jesus in death and for us. The inner reality of the Eucharist, however, is the Christ of Calvary continuing now, but in glorified form, the identical fullness of sacrificial self-offering that he achieved on Calvary.

Eucharist as Sacrament

In saying that liturgy joins God's saving presence with man's responsiveness, the point being made is that liturgy is worship. Worship is precisely the meeting of God and man in love: on the part of God a saving love, on the part of man a love of recognition, acceptance, and conversion. And in liturgy this takes place in the form of symbolic acts, acts which focus clearly the presence and initiative of God, and acts which suitably communicate man's recognition and due response.

It is only in liturgy that full and perfect worship takes place. In any other form worship, if it takes place at all, is only incomplete and partial. Apart from the mutual presence of God and man, and apart from symbolic acts expressive of this mutuality, there is only searching, invitation, or a disposition for worship, but there is no worship in the full sense of the word.

This, of course, is not to say that genuine worship must always be external and celebrated in community. Genuine worship can be simply interior and private. Always, though, worship must join in sign God's presence and man's due reaction, which in the case of interior worship takes place in the interior focusing of personal faith and fitting acts of personal response. In the case of private external worship this takes place in the recognition of God's presence in persons or things, and personal acts of response selected according to one's own sense of fittingness.

Full and perfect worship, however, will always be external and celebrated in community, since God never acts toward an individual in isolation from the community of men — God acts toward men in Christ, who is sent for all. The individual, in turn, never fully answers to God apart from his willing presence and participation in the community of those with whom he shares humanness — and Christ.

Seeing the sacramental or communion aspect of the Eucharist as liturgical worship is, again, perhaps the main thing that distinguishes recent and contemporary theology's discussion of this aspect of the Eucharist.

Recently theology tended to overdistinguish communion and sacrifice. The Mass was *offered*, and communion *received*. Distinct rituals, obligations, and practices grew up around each. The sacrifice was over and done with when the celebrant had communicated. Beyond that the Eucharist was real presence, first for the sake of communion, second for the sake of visits and adoration. The sacrifice was liturgy, since worship was thought mainly to be man's offering (with Christ) to God. Communion, on the other hand, was gift on the part of God and devotion on the part of man. In theory, liturgy was more important, but in practice, due especially to the intimacy of the Lord's presence and the greater worth of his actions toward men, communion held primacy.

In contemporary theology this inversion of values is corrected by a more emphatic linking of sacrament and sacrifice. As has been indicated earlier, Old Testament liturgy joined inseparably sacrifice and sacred meal. This was surely the case with the major liturgies, especially Passover upon which the Eucharist was based. Offering the sacrifice was complete only in and through participating in the ritual meal prepared from the victim or its symbolic substitute.

This unity of sacrifice and communion once so evident in the faith and practice of the Church is again being restored under the influence of contemporary theology. The One received in communion is again seen as precisely the Victim who has offered himself. The real presence is not simply Jesus the Lord, lover of men, but Jesus the Lamb standing always in sacrifice for the sake of men. To receive communion is precisely to participate in his self-offering.

Communion thus emerges again as liturgy and worship, not merely meeting and devotion. Communion is the presence and saving act of Christ brought to bear on the individual, and the individual recognizing, accepting, and appreciating. Communion is thus the sacrifice extended and projected, the sacrifice accomplishing in the one what it is set to do for the many. Communion is the sacrifice completed, the sacrifice's natural and organic end.

Transignification

The recasting of eucharistic theology by contemporary theologians has in great part been accepted enthusiastically. Its enriching of sacramental piety has been unmistakable. It has also led, however, to certain suspicions of unorthodoxy aroused by a misunderstanding of the idea "transignification" introduced into the discussion of the Eucharist by a number of European theologians.

What does this idea express? The heart of the matter is that the Eucharist means more than a mere "coming to be present" by Christ, even more than a mere "making present anew the priestly act of Calvary." The presence and sacrifice of Christ are, rather, for the sake of the Church: the Eucharist has a sanctifying purpose; Jesus makes himself present as self-gift, to be accepted and shared in by the people of God.

It is this purpose aspect that is expressed by the term "transignification." From one point of view the Eucharist is a sign of Christ's presence and priestly act (sacrifice). To concentrate merely on this "signification," as both theology and piety tended to do in recent centuries, is to concentrate on merely half the meaning of the Eucharist. There is a further "signification" to be considered, a *trans*-signification, which is that of the Eucharist's being presence and sacrifice for the sanctifying of the Church.

Seemingly many jumped to the conclusion that the theologians sponsoring this idea and term were attempting to "water down" the traditional teaching on "transubstantiation." Even the recent encyclical of Pope Paul (*Mysterium Fidei*) warned against any lessening of faith in the real change of bread and wine into the Body and Blood of Christ. Rather than lessening faith in this change, however, the theologians putting forth the idea of "transignification" are attempting to fill out, complete faith in it.

The point they make is that transubstantiation brings about merely the "sign" of Christ's presence and sacrificial act, but the further "purpose-sign" of transubstantiation has also to be considered, since Jesus comes to be in the Eucharist not just to be, but to sanctify.

A further aspect of transignification is that it relates the eucharistic presence and activity of Christ to the many other forms of his presence and activity in the Church and world. Vatican II, in its *Constitution on the Sacred Liturgy*, makes it very clear, for example, that Christ is already present and active in several ways in the liturgy prior to transubstantiation. This being so, it is necessary that theology relate these forms of presence and activity to the Eucharist. In all these forms Christ is present for the sake of sanctifying. In the Eucharist, however, it is his very self, his very priestly self-offering that is the Gift presented for sanctifying, not merely some form of his sanctifying power. Transignificance, therefore, reaches a climax with his eucharistic presence and activity, since the "signs" here indicate that it is his very Person offered for the life of the Church.

Readings

Bouyer, Louis, *History of Christian Spirituality* (New York: Desclee Co., 1963), Vol. I, Part 1.

O'Neill, Colman, O.P., *New Approaches to the Eucharist* (New York: Alba House, 1967).

Powers, Joseph M., S.J., *Eucharistic Theology* (New York: Herder & Herder, 1967).

Schoonenberg, Piet, "Eucharistic Presence," *Cross Currents*, Winter, 1967.

MARRIAGE

The difference between recent and contemporary theology with respect to marriage can be summed up in the differences between a contract and a commitment. There is a remarkable sameness about these two notions, but an equally remarkable difference. The one is almost exclusively legal in orientation, the other mainly personal. Under analysis what can be seen happening today is that the contractual nature of marriage is being set by contemporary theologians in a broader context. Emphasized today is the sacramental nature of marriage and the personal ends it is by nature and grace assigned to accomplish. This emphasis is in no way opposed to the former way of explaining marriage; it is, rather, an enrichment and refinement of that previous teaching.

Marriage as a Sacrament

Marriage is everything that humanity has always thought it is, and more: it is also what God has disclosed it to be. Central to this divine disclosure is that marriage is a sign of grace, a sacrament. Marriage is a love-relationship that signifies the presence of Christ's sanctifying charity. With the symbolic ritual of its celebration, marriage introduces its participants into a new and altogether special framework of holiness.

The unique gift sacramentally bestowed by marriage is a deeper sharing in the mystery of love-union that binds the Persons of the Blessed Trinity to one another. More immediately it is a deeper sharing in the love-union with God experienced in the humanity of Christ.

Sharing in this mystery is really the essence of sanctifying grace. What makes the sanctifying grace of marriage different is the mutuality of its deeper possession. Married persons are introduced into a deeper sharing in the love-union of the God-head not as individuals but as a couple. They are given grace with particular reference to one another. For this reason they henceforth relate to one another, as well as to God, other persons, and the world, not as I and Thou, but as We.

Like the Eucharist, marriage is also a continuing sacrament. Though celebrated in a moment, marriage is a sacramental reality that abides. It is an ever-present source of its own special gift. In whatever married persons engage having to do with their marriage the sacrament of marriage renews itself: the power of love-union is made more energetic, the bond of love-union more emphatic.

As with all sacraments, though, the grace-effectiveness of marriage, especially in its continuing aspect, will only be as actual as the partners really want it to be. There is nothing magic or automatic about the sacraments; they transform only what is really submitted to their sanctifying influence.

Marriage as a Charism

The gift of God in marriage is not confined to personal holiness. God also gives in marriage a particular grace of service: the conjugal charism. He endows married persons for a ministry. He consecrates them for a series of charity-tasks. To marry is to enter upon an office: it is to enter into a new and altogether special framework of responsibilities in the Lord.

It is well known, especially in light of recent theology, that married persons contract mutually to fulfill the responsibilities inherent to marriage itself. These responsibilities have been classically enumerated as procreating and rearing children, sharing conjugal love, extending mutual assistance, and supporting one another's weaknesses of the flesh. To these responsibilities married persons commit themselves together for life. These responsibilities are, in fact, their very life.

What contemporary theology adds to the understanding of these responsibilities is a clarifying of their relationship to the redeeming love of Christ. Contemporary theology emphasizes, in other words, yet another responsibility in marriage, that of bringing the conjugal community to the fullness of life in the Holy Spirit.

Marriage, then, is a *mission*, a collaborating with Christ in his sanctifying work. To possess the conjugal charism is to be *sent* by Christ as ministers of redeeming grace: to one another, to the children of the marital union, to the world surrounding and touching the conjugal community.

Married persons are thus called and endowed to be sacramental signs of healing grace for one another, their family, and their "world." They are to interpret and illustrate within the conjugal community and its social framework the ways and love of God. They are to translate the mystery of God's love into human forms. They are to reincarnate Christ by incarnating in their shared life his Holy Spirit.

Implicit here is an immense ideal, not so immense, however, as to surpass the charism designed for its achievement. The call and power given in marriage are precisely what originates and vitalizes the Church itself. Marriage, in fact, is the Church in miniature: Christ enlivening, unifying, healing, and energizing the community of God's people. At least marriage is meant to be this in virtue of the gifts it bequeaths to its participants.

Chief among its service-responsibilities is the need of marriage to stand before the Church as a facsimile of what the Church itself is supposed to be. Tradition has too long assigned this role exclusively to those in religious life. One dimension of the Church's life, however, is best expressed by married persons. To them the Church should look for the vision of shared love in the Spirit directed specifically to persons in the world and for the service of the world. Even religious should be able to look to married persons as the primary sign of Christ's love continuing among men.

Contemporary theology traces the sacramental and charismatic lines of marriage thus: marriage is a love-union between a man and a woman which as a sign of the mystery of the Church has as its total objective the perfecting of conjugal love in the Holy Spirit, and as its vital sources sanctifying grace and the conjugal charism. The total objective of marriage is rightly stated in terms of love since marriage anticipates a mutual state of mind and heart disclosing the partners as wholly given to the inherent responsibilities of marriage, and with a view to fulfilling these as perfectly as possible in the Holy Spirit. And though the deepest sources of this fulfillment are sacramental vitalities, these work themselves out and take expression only in continuing efforts toward unity and charity.

An Old Problem Revisited

One of the great social problems of the day is divorce. Its prevalence raises the question of the permanent character of marriage. An old question, for all its acuteness today, it is answered substantially the same by recent and contemporary theologians: marriage is essentially indissoluble, and divorce gives no right of remarriage. The question has a new wrinkle currently, however. Scholars and people are beginning seriously to wonder whether all the ingredients of valid marriage are really being considered with respect to divorce. Perchance many divorces are actually annulments, instances wherein actual marriage never took place, and are thus not suspensive of the right to "remarry." A serious look is also being given the history of Church practice, and again a difference is noted between East and West; it is also noted that even the West at one time concurred with the eastern practice of allowing real divorce with right of remarriage.

Indissolubility

Friendship engages our mind, our talents, our feelings — portions of our being. Marriage, on the other hand, engages our whole being: we communicate in marriage with our entire person.

Underlying and giving rise to marriage, then, is the fact of our being persons sexually diversified. Were there no sex there would be only friendship between persons. With sex there is marriage.

The mystery of sex consists in its stamping man and woman as open to a certain totality of personal union, a union far surpassing that made possible by the mere fact of their being persons. Tradition has for this total union the special name *marital union.*

When a man and woman marry they are in search of that union which the sexuality of their personal nature makes possible. This, in fact, is the union they pledge to one another: they specifically vow to each other everything required to make marital union a reality between themselves. What this amounts to is a totality of human love and mutual responsibility, both for one another and the purposes inherent to their complete sharing of life.

There is something about this that is of its nature perpetual and irrevocable. We do not make friends simply for a weekend; friendship is a process that envisions neither termination nor recall. Marriage is even more permanent.

The love that urges marriage looks to fullness. It takes stock neither of time nor degree. The only restrictions it knows are those inherent to love itself. In tendency and objective it envisions a lifetime. For genuine love to motivate a *trial* marriage or one of restricted duration seems completely a contradiction.

Thus, the so-called *personal ends* of marriage themselves indicate the inadmissibility of divorce with right of remarriage. To rupture the marital union, even though it be as yet unfulfilled, and to reclaim the right of giving oneself *totally* to another (how can one give oneself *totally* to more than one person?) contradicts the very nature of the love-union made possible by sex and implied in the marriage vows.

Here we find unmistakable support for the traditional Christian rejection of divorce with right of remarriage. Not that the teaching of Christ needs our support; several contemporary studies, especially that of Father Edward Schillebeeckx, leave no doubt that the Christian revelation condemns total divorce. The reasonableness of this condemnation is seen, nonetheless, in the very nature of marital love.

The reasonableness of this is also seen in the fact that marital love, being total, involves the use of sex, which carries with it an implicit responsibility for the fruit of that use. Not that marital sexuality must always be procreative. It must, though, be concerned with marital love, and the only restrictions love allows are those looking to the real good of the love-union itself. All things being equal, marital love will seldom dictate a perpetual deferring of procreative sexuality.

The use of sex, then, presumes a stable framework into which the fruit of that use can be introduced and nurtured, which is an obvious requirement until parental responsibilities have been completely fulfilled. Thus parental love reinforces the indissolubility of marriage arising from the total nature of marital love.

Indissolubility, however, is primarily held on faith rather than rational argument. It is the word of Christ that verifies this quality in marriage. Nor was he being merely arbitrary. Rather than inventing marriage, he took it for what it was meant to be by his Father, and in light of that designated it to serve as a sign of his own union with his Church. Marriage is indissoluble because it is meant to be a sacrament.

Divorce

But what of the countless remarriages today — are they all invalid? And what of the many divorced persons who in conscience are claiming themselves exceptions to the traditional Christian teaching and practice? And what exactly is the traditional Christian practice with respect to divorce and remarriage?

Today the Church is recognizing more clearly, first of all, that many cases of "divorce" deal with individuals who were simply inadequate psychologically for marriage in the first place. For these, in other words, it is not so much a matter of divorce as of annulment.

Some writers are suggesting today that the Church also begin paying more attention, first, to the kind of knowledge required for marriage, and second, to the kind of sexuality required for sealing or consummating a marriage. On both scores, these writers suggest, many more divorce cases would be resolved in terms of annulment.

As for requisite knowledge, they suggest that many hasty and early marriages that end in divorce would, if examined closely, reveal a lack of that understanding necessary for embracing marriage in its *total* meaning. Regarding sexuality, they suggest that unless it be a real expression of marital love, as distinct from mere physical activity, it too is not sufficient for sealing a marriage irrevocably.

The problem with these suggestions, for all that they may well be correct, is that they deal with what is practically impossible to prove. And the judging of whether a marriage exists or not begs for proof. One possible approach is that the Church feel its way toward a greater honoring of the testimony, under oath, of the person(s) involved. This would be a person-centeredness on the part of the Church, in itself wholly admirable, but rife with all the consequences of human error, weakness, and even malice. The Church will quite rightly, therefore, move only slowly and cautiously in that direction.

That all her members will move so slowly and cautiously is another matter. Already there are indications that many who in conscience regard their marriage certainly invalid but legally unprovable are being counseled to do in conscience what seems best for them, be that in terms of receiving the sacraments — provided scandal is not given — while in an "invalid" second marriage, or entering into a "second" marriage itself. We deal here with an area where the limits of human law fall short of all the human realities that can enter a legal situation. It is a painful area, wherein only God can judge. A charitable suspending of accusation is in order, therefore, and a humble willingness to be guided by those bearing the greater responsibility for the well-being of God's people.

Further understanding may follow from a continuing study of the history of the Church's practice regarding divorce. Some thinkers today are convinced that in the past, both in the East and West, the Church exercised a discreet and pastorally-motivated tolerance of divorce and remarriage. This practice, moreover, was neither considered a betrayal of the gospel nor an undermining of the common good. The indissolubility of marriage was taken to mean that married partners could not themselves break their commitment, but that Christ, the apostles, or the Church could judge the commitment broken by actual or equivalent divorce in certain instances. With respect to this more study is needed and, again, caution is greatly in order. A continuing renewal of the Church, however, might well lead to a fuller understanding and reactivation of the pastoral sensitivities of both the gospel and the Church's earliest teachers.

Readings

Abbott & Gallagher (eds.), *Pastoral Constitution on the Church in the Modern World*, in *The Documents of Vatican II* (New York: Guild Press, 1966), Part 2, Chap. 1.

America, February 7, 1968 — Special issue on Marriage, Divorce, and Canon Law.

Bird, Joseph D., and Lois F., *Freedom of Sexual Love* (Garden City, N. Y.: Doubleday, 1967).

Ford, John, S.J., and Kelly, Gerald, S.J., *Contemporary Moral Theology, Vol. 2: Marriage Questions* (Westminster, Md.: Newman, 1963).

Häring, Bernard, C.Ss.R., *A Sacramental Spirituality* (New York: Sheed & Ward, 1962), Chap. 13.

Oraison, Marc, *The Human Mystery of Sexuality* (New York: Sheed & Ward, 1967).

Pospishil, Victor J., *Divorce and Remarriage* (New York: Herder & Herder, 1967).

Schillebeeckx, Edward, O.P., *Marriage — Human Reality and Saving Mystery* (New York: Sheed & Ward, 1965).

PART FIVE

Basic Moral Elements

GRACE

The study of grace has had a long history. It has had, in fact, two long histories: one in the West, another in the East. Perhaps no other part of theology has had such a varied background.

By the same token, no other part of theology has been more profitably re-examined in this era of doctrinal renewal. The main features of the western and eastern traditions on grace have been gathered together, and the result is a most happy enrichment of the Church's understanding.

Historical Developments

Thought on grace in the western Church is mainly traceable to St. Augustine. It was the contribution of this great saint to explain grace as a source of Godlike activity. Due to his influence, seeing grace as a source of Christian living, as a power that makes Christian actions possible, became the main feature of the western tradition.

Augustine made his point against Pelagius, who maintained that a life holy and pleasing to God was quite possible without grace.

Perceiving in the Pelagian line of thought a denial of the universal and crippling effect of original sin, Augustine countered with his concept of grace as a new and second nature. His concern was with sanctifying grace, that gift of God whereby persons become adopted children of God. For all practical purposes, however, his thinking dealt with actual grace, the power whereby God enables persons already his adopted children so to act as to win his favor and rewards.

The clear distinction between sanctifying and actual grace was really the contribution of later theologians, especially those of the thirteenth and sixteenth centuries. By that time, though, the action-emphasis in the western understanding of grace was too pronounced to allow for any other consideration of grace than as an empowerment for Christian behavior.

After the sixteenth century, in fact, grace was explained almost entirely in terms of God's moving a person's free will to choose good and holy actions. Among the regrettable results of this was the preoccupation of theologians — and catechisms as well — with the unanswerable and quite unnecessary problem of harmonizing the power of grace and human freedom.

In the East things developed differently. Though they had their problems, the theologians of Antioch and Alexandria were never bothered by a person like Pelagius. Neither were they fascinated, as were their western peers, by practicality.

The eastern mind was — and remains — contemplative and mystical. As the eastern fathers were absorbed by the Trinity rather than the Unity of God, by the divinity rather than the humanity of Christ, so they were enthralled by the gift-aspect of grace rather than its power-aspect.

As they read the Scriptures, grace was to be explained as God's very giving of himself in loving relationship. Grace, they taught, is everything — even creation — that issues from God's love, but especially the Holy Spirit himself through whose presence and holiness persons are changed. And the change in question is not so much that of being empowered for holy actions as being given to share life, to have fellowship with the all-holy Father, Son, and Spirit. To describe this change the eastern theologians spoke of a person's being "divinized" and "transformed."

With little alteration this is the emphasis that has continued in the eastern Churches even to the present day. Quite obviously the stress is on sanctifying grace, that feature of God's self-gift which is a person's re-creation, or, as Greek Christians would probably say, his fuller creation in the image of God's own holiness. More specifically, the stress is on what St. Thomas and the western theologians have called "uncreated" grace, God himself in self-giving.

Renewal

This at least is the way Matthias Scheeben understood the eastern fathers in his pioneering studies on the renewal of the theology of grace published late in the past century. He had, as it were, "rediscovered" the Greek tradition, and the result was a reshuffling of the whole direction of western thinking on grace. In place of actual grace, sanctifying grace was given primacy of importance. And beyond sanctifying grace, God's very self-gift, grace in the fullest sense of the word, won primacy.

This in turn led to studies on the matter that surpass even the theology of the Blessed Trinity for depth and complexity. The most celebrated name in this connection is that of Maurice de la Taille (pronounced *tie*), a French theologian of the 1920's who envisioned grace as God's awakening in man wholly new depths of humanness. At the present time Prudentius de Letter writes extensively in this same vein.

Though hardly against theological speculations, Peter Fransen advises a toning down of this depth analysis of grace. Its continuance, he admonishes, endangers missing the whole point of the mystery of grace which is essentially a relationship between persons. Theologians, he implies, seldom get beyond considering the conditions upon which that relationship rests, and by so doing foster more interest in the "mechanics" of grace than in grace itself.

This appears to be the general mood of writings on grace today, a mood greatly supported by biblical studies. The Scriptures do not so much analyze grace as present the realities that go together to comprise the extensive mystery that we call grace. The mood is that of reawakening appreciation for this mystery, above all of deepening participation in it.

Grace and Nature

Theologians will be theologians, however, and in spite of the mood to the contrary they continue to probe the mystery for understanding. One of the most fruitful areas of research has been that of the relationship between grace and human nature.

Under the influence of St. Augustine, western theology came to regard grace as a kind of addition to creation. First God made man, whole and complete in humanness; then he added grace, elevating man by that addition to a new and higher state of being, power, and destiny.

Modern theologians tend to dislike this approach. It makes grace even more difficult to understand than it already is, they say, and seems to have God creating two worlds, that of creation and that of grace. Since grace touches man so deeply, modern theologians think another explanation of grace is possible, one that brings human nature and grace into a more realistic unity.

Starting with the traditional teaching that grace is first of all man's being called to eternal life, these theologians envision grace fundamentally as the possibility of eternal life bequeathed by God in the very act of man's creation.

Man, they explain, has never existed for any other ultimate purpose but eternal life in communion with the Blessed Trinity. His humanness has never had an intended destiny other than this. That man can never achieve his only real destiny of eternal life except through grace, however, does not of itself mean that he had first to be created and only then given the possibility of achieving that destiny. This possibility, rather, can be regarded as part and parcel of his being from the beginning.

This surely is in keeping with the intuitions of eastern theology, both ancient and contemporary. Creation, for eastern thinkers, is the physical realization of God's sole purpose: to begin the process of man's coming to complete sharing of life with himself in his majestic Trinity.

First, then, modern thinkers tend to hold that man was *called* to eternal life in the very act of creation. His being was "bent toward" or "shaped for" eternal life, not by the fact of his humanness, but by the fact of a special possibility "built into" his humanness by God from the beginning.

But the call is not enough. There has also to be a possibility of *response*, the possibility of fulfilling the call. This too was given, but again, in the act of creation, not as a later addition.

What this means is that man's humanness was from the start "energized" by God himself for life in process toward fullness of beatific communion with the Trinity. Man, in a word, never existed in possession of the powers of humanness alone. Rather, from the beginning he was possessed of a humanness "charged" with possibilities of achieving life with God. And these possibilities were born directly of God's special presence to him and activity in him, a presence and activity likewise associated with the very act of creation.

This line of thought has not been proposed without contest. In 1950, for example, the encyclical of Pius XII, *Humani Generis*, cautioned against any teaching that threatened a "watering down" of the distinction between grace and humanness. Especially it cautioned against any insinuation that grace is not so much a free gift as something due to man's being.

Such a warning was not lost on theologians. It had the effect, in fact, of practically terminating public thought on the matter for about a decade. With the advent of Vatican II, however, especially the spirit of open inquiry it inaugurated in the Church, theologians again returned to the topic. And they found further grist for their thinking mills in the "process" thought of the day, the continuing biblical studies, and the widening influence of eastern theology.

Today they tend to be satisfied that the conditions imposed by *Humani Generis* can be met while still regarding grace and humanness as a unity. They explain that the coincidence of grace and humanness from the beginning does not imply that they had to coincide; grace remains, in other words, a complete gift. Neither does it follow that because man's real destiny is eternal life both the call and response regarding that destiny are essential ingredients of humanness as such; the difference between grace and humanness, in other words, remains intact. Grace, therefore, can safely be regarded as bequeathed to man in the very act of creation. He was neither created without it, nor is he capable of his real life process without it.

Implications For Humanness

One implication of this is that man is "supernatural" in the depths of his being from the word "go." And he never loses this. The call to eternal life, the first installment of grace, can never be lost, even in sin. This, in fact, is what makes sin so terrible for man: remaining called to the fullness of life, a person lives in a state of refusing to heed that call. Substitutes for that fullness can only postpone the inevitable frustration that is the bitter fruit of unrepented sin.

On the positive side, this call to eternal life is the basis for man's every good act contributing to his achieving eternal life. To his call corresponds the power of response, the second installment of grace. There is no such thing as mere "natural" response: there is grace or there is sin, nothing else. Everyone of good purpose, therefore, is in grace, is being "saved," whether this be perceived through faith or not. And by the same token everything of good purpose is a "sign" of grace, no matter how dimly.

More positive still is the further implication that grace works in and through man's humanness for the sake of ever fuller *humanness*. To be sure, grace fashions man as a special image of God. Always, though, it leaves man in the realm of *image*. It is his humanness that is enriched, that takes on Godlike aspects. Grace is a power for human development and achievement. Working at the center of our being, it opens us to new and greater human possibilities.

Rather than driving him to live above, apart from, or in spite of the world, therefore, grace urges man to be ever more in and of the world. He is a participant in its very process of "becoming," and is in fact the responsible image-agent of its temporal achievement. As everything of good purpose "graces" man, so man's every good purpose "graces" the world.

When possessed of faith, the refinement of grace in man's mind, or of hope and especially of love, the refinements of grace in his will, this reciprocal influence of man and world is wholly special. The Christian is uniquely responsible for the world and is in turn uniquely served by the world. Ultimately this interrelated process is meant to culminate in the transforming of both, of the world at least in time, and of man in eternity. In both cases the product will be that of grace, but achieved in and through an enriched humanness.

Readings

Fortman, Edmund J., S.J., *The Theology of Man and Grace: Commentary* (Milwaukee: Bruce, 1966).

Fransen, Peter, *Divine Grace and Man* (New York: New American Library, 1965).

Gleason, Robert W., S.J., *Grace* (New York: Sheed & Ward, 1962).

Journet, Charles, *The Meaning of Grace* (New York: Paulist Press, 1962).

Kenny, J. P., S.J., "Reflections on Human Nature and the Supernatural," *Theological Studies*, June, 1953.

Rahner, Karl, S.J., *Nature and Grace* (New York: Sheed & Ward, 1964).

Stevens, Gregory, O.S.B., *The Life of Grace* (Englewood Cliffs, N. J.: Prentice-Hall, 1963).

LAW

As an ingredient of Christian life, law is an extraordinarily complex reality. It embraces natural law, grace, the moral teachings of Jesus and the Church, ecclesiastical and civil law, domestic directives such as are laid down by parents and schools, and conscience.

Some of these have the nature of law in the usual sense, others in a different sense. Grace, domestic directives, and conscience are of the latter kind, and have been or will be treated elsewhere. Natural, ecclesiastical, and civil law, which have the nature of law in the usual sense, will be treated here, and will be set in relation to the moral teachings of Jesus and the Church. On each of these recent and contemporary theology differ widely.

Natural Law

Of all the areas of recent theology none has been subjected to more criticism today than its teaching on natural law.

At the heart of that teaching is a definition of natural law as the combination of moral responsibilities and freedoms which are grounded in and issue from human nature seen in the light of its essential "parts" and relationships. The definition is complex and its explanation difficult even for experts.

First to be noted is that the recent teaching centered on common or general humanness, not on the individual. It considered human nature as it is commonly composed of spiritual and physical elements, and as it is the subject of general relationships with God, men, and things. Of specific concern were the common responsibilities and freedoms stemming from its possession.

Because human nature implies a rational soul, a person was said to be charged with using and developing his mind and will. Because it implies a physical body, one had to use and maintain his organism according to the needs and purposes of its parts.

Human nature was known to be created and the subject of salvation, and for this reason a person was obliged to cultivate relationship with God. Similarly, regarding other men: as common possessors of human nature they were owed justice and charity, a relationship insuring respect of their equality and uniqueness. Things of the world, standing always in reference to persons, had also to be approached and used in light of that reference; otherwise the just claims and needs of human nature would be ignored.

Second to be noted is that the recent teaching led to a widespread understanding of all man's fundamental responsibilities and freedoms as "packaged" into his being, to be "unwrapped" for every situation by logical thought. The mind was to read and the will to follow a built-in blueprint of all right decisions.

Against this understanding modern thinkers react strongly. One of these is Germain Grisez. His explanation of natural law, which he presents as that of St. Thomas Aquinas, releases both mind and will from subjection to any preprogrammed plan of behavior.

Natural law, he says, is but the sum of man's basic tendencies toward human well-being. Some of these tendencies simply have to be fulfilled, others are a matter of choice. Regarding all of them, however, a person is free as to their manner of fulfillment. The only law they imply is that they be not contradicted; to act against them is to act against oneself, which is to violate intelligence and freedom.

Grisez places the determining of human well-being precisely in the hands of each person and subjects him to only one prohibition. In so doing he remedies a tendency in the recent teaching to be far more clear on prohibitions than on the fulfilling of positive goals.

Other reputable contemporary thinkers go further than Grisez. Their complaint is that the recent teaching failed to consider human nature's evolving and individualized aspects. The full richness of human nature only gradually surfaces, they explain, a process furthered by changing historical and cultural conditions. In the case of woman, marriage, and war, as was noted earlier when discussing *process*, human nature is experienced differently today. With each such experience the scope of natural law should be seen to shift.

This shifting process does not lead to a contradiction of previously grasped responsibilities. Typically it leads to a discovery of additional responsibilities. These, however, have to be integrated with those previously grasped, which may result in a modifying of the latter. Actually, rather than their being modified, they are simply more adequately understood.

Contemporary thinkers also lean heavily on the fact that human nature exists only in individual form. What this implies is that a person is held only to such responsibilities as arise from his own particular humanness. And here too humanness surfaces only gradually.

That each person shares common responsibilities with other men is undeniable. Common responsibilities, however, are but features of the responsibilities and freedoms proper to a person's individuality. It is only one's own humanness, not that of all men or of one's neighbor, that is the real natural law.

As for theology and natural law, modern theologians like Josef Fuchs, Karl Rahner, and Henri de Lubac see human nature and grace far more intertwined than recent theologians. Grace is seen as a level of "possibility" in human nature that opens a person toward God, men, and things in a way wholly in harmony with God's ultimate purposes.

This obviously has implications for natural law. Only human nature as graced, individuality as graced, is the real source of those tendencies that look to man's consummate well-being. Only in virtue of grace do a person's fullest responsibilities and fullest freedoms surface in his humanness. In virtue of grace, then, natural law becomes Christian law.

The Moral Teachings of Jesus and the Church

Except for a few positive directives, such as believing in himself, accepting his message from his Church, and sharing in his mystery through baptism, the Eucharist, and other sacraments, it is difficult to find the precise contributions of Jesus in terms of law. Fathers Fuchs and Schnackenburg agree that Jesus presupposed his hearers' ability to know the whole body of natural law requirements. John L. McKenzie sees the commandment to love as the only new law that Jesus imposed on his followers. Jacques Leclercq wonders even about the "newness" of this, since love was a prominent theme in the message of religious teachers centuries before Jesus.

As with requirements, so with prohibitions one finds an ambiguity. Neither Jesus nor St. Paul indicated any specifically new prohibitions. They ratified those already known in virtue of the Old Law or the law written on human hearts. Only the rejection of Jesus himself or of those directives that look specifically to incorporating believers into his Church have anything like the ring of newness about them.

What emerges from this is that the New Law is nothing other than Jesus himself: commitment to him in faith, and participation in him through life in his Church. With this commitment and participation comes sharing his Holy Spirit, whose impulse is to draw from Christians ever more genuine signs of likeness to Christ. The heart of this likeness is an unconditional and ever-expanding life of love: doing everything good out of love and avoiding everything evil out of love. What is good and what is evil is known partly through the teaching of Jesus, partly from the reflections of the Church, partly from the understanding of mankind as a whole, and partly from the insights of personal conscience.

Rudolph Schnackenburg is emphatic in stating that it pertains to the Church to guide Christians and such men as will hear her in solving the moral and social problems that arise from decade to decade. But this involves more than the Church's consulting the New Testament. Jesus called all to the complete fulfillment of God's will, and he illustrated in word and deed what this could look like in practice; but as for knowing God's will, he left this in great part to the intelligence and research of men.

Consequently, though in possession of the insights and values incorporated in the New Testament and expanded with the history of theology, the Church must ever approach the problems of each era in real search of practical solutions. There is no such thing as its being in possession of ready-made answers to all mankind's problem at any given moment in history. For further word on this one need but consult Vatican II's *Constitution on the Church in the Modern World.*

Ecclesiastical Law

If the Church must struggle with problems arising from its being situated in the world, it must also struggle with problems arising from the very fact that it is a community of persons. It is because the Church is a community that it needs and possesses legislative authority and a system of laws.

If recent theology assigned a prominence to Church law not found in contemporary theology it was because Church law itself was more prominent in the life of the Church. Recent theology simply took this for granted, and explained the prevalence of laws as a necessary and meaningful determination of the Christian life.

One result of this passivity of recent theology was a widespread impression that Christian living meant little more than following the laws of the Church; all was thought well if one faithfully followed the Church's laws. Another result was a sophisticated process of legal hair-splitting to win release from laws.

Minimalism and legalism, then, are two of the main complaints that contemporary theology lodges against recent theology's treatment of Church law. More positively, contemporary theologians endeavor to explain the role of Church law in relation to the gospel.

Ecclesiastical laws, they insist, do not in any sense specify the fullness of Christian living. They specify, rather, the minimum: the minimum of worship, of ascetical practice, of good order and morality, of justice and charity. What laws imply is that, short of the minimum observance, the Church as a whole can only be said to be not responding, not appreciating, not using the gifts Christ has bestowed. Any effort on the part of Church legislators to determine by law the fullness of Christian responsiveness, therefore, is to betray the gospel. The Christian life of the individual, in fact, only *begins* with the minimum standards laid upon the entire community.

Another point with contemporary theologians is that law is but one technique at the Church's disposal for safeguarding and promoting Christian living. In the present day, moreover, it is a far less effective technique than disclosing the appeal of Christian ideals by word and deed. A mere removing of law is no technique, but a replacing of law with a more personal, simple, and scholarly proclaiming and illustrating of the gospel-life is.

As for release from the law, contemporary theologians are concerned, first, with reassessing the relative seriousness of particular laws, and second, with updating the understanding of what justly excuses from particular legal observances. The heart of their concern is the realization that the purpose of ecclesiastical law is to promote life in the mystery of Christ. In light of this, countless circumstances which were either not conceived or not appreciated by recent moralists are seen to make release from laws more spiritually significant than a frightened legal conformity. The point is not a disregard of laws, but a more personal and theological application of laws.

Unlike their recent counterparts, contemporary theologians also challenge the wisdom of retaining certain particular laws. Their approach is based on the clear realization that most ecclesiastical laws are essentially related to historical situations, having value solely in light of the situations occasioning them. Adjusting Church laws to new situations is seen to be a serious responsibility both of Church legislators and those teaching and applying these laws.

Civil Law

Perhaps more than elsewhere the attitudes of minimalism and legalism unwittingly promoted by recent theology manifested themselves in the area of civil law. In theory, recent theology assigned the same validity to civil legislation as it did to the laws of the Church. In practice, however, it preferred to think that, unlike the Church, the state usually laid insupportable burdens on the citizenry. Theory and practice were harmonized in the celebrated notion of "purely penal" laws: laws dealing with matters not of themselves disruptive of good order or natural law oblige only to the paying of the penalty, not to their observance as such.

Against this idea contemporary theologians prefer to think that civil law binds in conscience in the same way as every other instance of valid law. Their seriousness on the point is balanced, however, by an equal seriousness regarding the norms for interpreting and applying laws. If civil laws be unjust, whether by undue multiplication or disregard of basic rights, they simply do not oblige, neither to observance nor to penalty. At times the greater law of good order or responsibility to others will bind one to their observance or penalty, as the case may be. By the same token, however, the greater law of the common good or the dignity of the human person will bind one at times to responsible civil disobedience.

The point here is that, in both foundation and fact, civil law is taken seriously by contemporary theologians, so seriously that maneuvers to acknowledge its legitimacy while avoiding its claim on conscience are soundly rejected.

Readings

Boyle, Paul M., C.P., "The Relationship of Law to Love," *Jurist*, 25 (1965), October, pp. 393–406.

Curran, Charles E., *Christian Morality Today* (Notre Dame, Ind.: Fides, 1966).

Drinkwater, F. H., *Birth Control and Natural Law* (Baltimore: Helicon, 1965).

Dupre, Louis, *Contraception and Catholics* (Baltimore, Helicon, 1964).

Fuchs, Josef, S.J., *Natural Law — A Theological Investigation* (New York: Sheed & Ward, 1965).

Grisez, Germain G., *Contraception and the Natural Law* (Milwaukee: Bruce, 1964), Chap. 3.

Leclercq, Jacques, *Christ and the Modern Conscience* (New York: Sheed & Ward, 1962).

McKenzie, John L., S.J., *Authority in the Church* (New York: Sheed & Ward, 1966).

———— "Law in the New Testament," paper read at Canon Law Society meeting, Chicago, October, 1965.

Monden, Louis, S.J., *Sin, Liberty and Law* (New York: Sheed & Ward, 1965).

Ranwez, E., "The Three Evangelical Counsels," in *Spirituality in Church and World*, Concilium No. 9 (New York: Paulist Press, 1965).

Schnackenburg, Rudolph, *The Moral Teaching of the New Testament* (New York: Herder & Herder, 1965).

CONSCIENCE

In recent centuries the theology of conscience has had two lead ideas, that conscience is an act of judgment, and that with it one discovers the moral nature of free acts. The first idea aimed at keeping conscience a thing of the mind rather than of the feelings. The second aimed at keeping it an internal "statement" of God's will corresponding to the external "statement" of that will in the gospel, human nature, the Church, and civil law.

Contemporary theology broadens both these ideas. It brings to them the notion of evaluative knowledge and fundamental option. It also lays stress on individuality, freedom, process, and grace to a degree unknown in recent theology.

Evaluative Knowledge

It is one thing to know what a thing means and another to know what it means for oneself. This in general is a distinction psychologists make between *notional* and *evaluative* knowledge, and contemporary theologians lean heavily on it. Conscience, the latter conclude, is an evaluative judgment.

Evaluative knowledge is more than mere mind. It is understanding, to be sure, but of how a thing implicates oneself. It is understanding joined with personal reactions: feelings, anxieties, desires.

If it concern a matter of practical morality, the reactions will be those of perceiving oneself responsible. Such a state may be worrisome or peaceful, sensing oneself under obligation or free of duty. The point is that one experiences the bond between the moral issue at hand and himself. And except for this experience a real judgment of conscience will not be made.

Fundamental Option

What is the basis of evaluative moral knowledge? To this

question recent theology answered: the use of reason. Having reached the age of reason a person can henceforth judge the relationship between his free acts and objective moral standards. Because he can reason he is responsible.

Contemporary theologians see little in this but a capacity for *notional* moral knowledge. The ability to reason and know moral standards, they note, does not mean one will see the reference those standards have to himself. Some other factor — a fundamental option — enables him to see this.

Ordinarily conscience is a judgment made in the light of a prior commitment. This commitment is the result of a choice one has made as to the meaning or goal of his life. By free decision he has given his life an ultimate direction and has committed himself to its pursuit.

Initially this is but an accepting of the moral direction one finds himself moving in at first maturity. It is made freely but mainly spontaneously, without crisis. Later with greater awareness it will be repeated or reversed, even many times, and often with suffering.

Both its initial and later form(s) denote a person committed to something around which his life's meaning revolves. This makes him a moral subject, a person of conscience. His judgments henceforth "monitor" his decisions: he judges these to be faithful or contradictory to his life-purpose.

Why does a person make a fundamental option? Here contemporary theologians give practically the same answer that recent theologians gave for the very fact of conscience. Persons do this because they are human beings: they must give themselves totally to something that promises fulfillment. Ultimately their choice is between seeking God or themselves. With the choice, though, they are responsible to themselves as committed, and must judge and make decisions accordingly.

Decisions and Acts

The basic commitment of a person takes expression in subsequent decisions and acts. These may be consistent or inconsistent with that commitment. At times they may express its contradiction and reversal. The point is that they never have personal meaning except in relation to a person's basic commitment. Apart from that relation, decisions and acts are mere "shells," motions, one might say, that are capable of "carrying" personal meaning but here and now do not.

In recent centuries theology was preoccupied with the relation of decisions and acts with human nature and laws. It was little concerned with a person's fundamental commitment. Its interest was objective morality, not personal morality.

This interest led to a detailed understanding of what actions naturally lend themselves to conveying a commitment to authentic moral values and what actions serve to convey a contradiction of those values. By the same token it led to making personal morality almost wholly a matter of deciding for or against the placing of certain actions. It made personal morality action-centered rather than commitment-centered.

While claiming and exercising the right to re-evaluate, contemporary theology tends to accept recent theology's list of essentially good and intrinsically evil acts. Its preoccupation, however, is personal morality. It is interested in decisions and acts as actual bearers of personal morality, not as mere moral "shells."

Contemporary theologians refuse to find sin or virtue solely in decisions made or acts placed. They find it in the meaning given these by the person. And they are more interested in a pattern or series of decisions and acts. Individual decisions and acts tell very little of a person's basic moral commitment, whereas a pattern tells much.

Process and Freedom

Contemporary theology is also preoccupied with conscience as a subject of growth. Decisions and acts stem from a whole variety of moral moods and moments of growth. Only gradually do they take on a consistent reflection of a person's basic moral commitment.

And even one's basic moral commitment is subject to process. Only gradually does awareness of one's life-direction emerge from the shadows of infancy. Even more gradually does an ability to make a firm choice in the matter emerge. A total moral commitment is possible *only* after a long process of self-discovery and evaluative understanding.

Mortal sin is a case in point. Contemporary theology sees mortal sin as a personal reversal of a basic commitment to God and the things of God. It is one of a person's deepest decisions, involving complete self-donation akin to marrying, coming to faith, or taking vows.

Those decisions and acts which recent theology assessed as contradictory of their nature to God's purposes are not decisions and acts one engages in casually or routinely. Their very seriousness begs for previous consideration, since willing them is to endorse their contradictory character as one's own purpose.

A morally immature person simply cannot bring to such decisions and acts the necessary depth of consideration and willingness. A morally mature person, on the other hand, simply does not do so, if he is not sufficiently self-possessed or free to make their contradictory nature wholly symbolic or expressive of his own reversal of commitment to God.

For its very seriousness, therefore, mortal sin is rare. It is even nonexistent where contradictory decisions and acts are symptoms of a conscientious struggle to find and maintain a basic commitment to God.

Regarding one's basic moral commitment and the decisions and acts related to it a person is and must remain free. He can be directed even firmly, with respect to both; but fundamentally, whether he be old or young, his life of conscience is his own affair.

And his freedom, too, is a process. A total commitment, be it to selfless morality or to selfishness, requires maturity. To mature is gradually to win release from internal and/or external influences that shackle one's ability to hold and give himself freely. Prior to initial maturity one is in search of a basic commitment; his moral life is a series of isolated acts in which he is at most only partially involved.

Recent theology tended to regard moral freedom as the rule whereas contemporary theology tends to regard it as the exception. At least contemporary theologians do not make moral freedom coextensive with the use of reason. It is, rather, an inner stature that has to be "created" through struggle for growth. And persons differ widely in this respect.

Spirit and Situation

For furthering this process of growth the grace and guidance of the Holy Spirit is the main influence, according to contemporary theologians. It was not otherwise with recent theologians, though there was a difference.

For recent theology, the objective of conscience was the personal discovery of the moral requirements resting on all men. The Spirit of God was said to guide the person in this, both as to discovery and acceptance. That the Spirit would guide an individual, within the framework of common requirements, to a pattern of special requirements was, again, thought to be the exception. Such a situation was regarded as the lot of a saint, and called for a special body of directions, to say nothing of directors.

Contemporary theology will have none of this. Individual guidance of the Spirit is meant to be the rule, not the exception. Individuality embodies God's will as much as common requirements. Discovering oneself internally and socially is a responsibility basic to each person. Meeting this responsibility, and especially giving oneself fully to the further responsibilities born of one's individuality and life-situation, is a process begging for the light and support of the Spirit every step of the way. Saints are but individuals with a richer individuality and life-situation than others, richer, that is, in conscience-requirements. Their moral process, however, is of the same fabric as that of all individuals.

A question arising today is whether a person is ever called by God to act in conscience contrary to the common requirements resting on all men. This is the question of "situation ethics," surely, because of its pervasive implications, the most important moral question of our time.

To this question the principles of recent theology offer a resounding negative. Preoccupied with common requirements, those principles hold little significance for individual requirements, especially where the latter seem to run counter to the former.

Contemporary theology looks at this question more openly, at least more in light of the individual; but it has not as yet completed its answer. Of several things it is certain. It is certain, for example, that an individual can be required by God to make and pursue a commitment which within the framework of common requirements asks more of him than others. It is certain, too, that an individual can be called to witness against a false or inadequate understanding of common requirements, especially those based on outmoded human laws and traditions.

It is not at all certain, however, that God would ever call a person to decisions or acts that contradict valid and authentic common requirements. Its sympathies are with those mistaken on the matter but its judgment is against them. It is being suggested, nonetheless, that in certain moral situations of extraordinary complexity and seriousness, one may have simply to do what one can, choosing one value rather than another while remaining sincerely devoted to both. Since not all moral values can be pursued at once, even when several call for response simultaneously, some situations may well require a choice of one and a deferral of another. Whether this line of thought will gradually clarify and prevail remains to be seen.

A key to this problem may lie in theology's gradual realization that certainty regarding the nature and extent of certain controversial common requirements — for example, the prohibition against contraception and falsehood — is not as available as recent theology believed. In this process the judgment of individual consciences will doubtless play an important role, as will the thinking of those following other moral traditions than that of the Catholic Church. For Catholics, nonetheless, the prudential guidance of the Church will be of critical significance. It will be, in fact, the main balancing factor between the notional insights of individuals and their evaluative judgments of conscience.

Social Horizons

Recent theology and even much of what has been outlined here on contemporary theology lends itself to an overly individualistic understanding of the life of conscience. A failure to note the essentially social horizon of conscience would be a serious one.

Vatican II made it unmistakably clear that a person is not

meeting the full call of God today by an exclusive formation of conscience in terms of one's individual humanness and immediate surroundings. Surely the responsibilities of our being and immediate relationships body forth God's purposes. But so do the needs of all men and the "creative" possibilities of modern times. A truly formed conscience detects God's will both in his personal world and in the world at large, and finds ways of answering to both.

Those with a basic commitment to moral goodness, therefore, must today more than ever be willing to expand the scope of that commitment far beyond a mere "saving of their souls." Those being guided toward a fundamental moral commitment must energetically be led to identify their cause with God's purposes for the whole of mankind. With respect to this, Section 30 of Chapter Two of the *Constitution on the Church in the Modern World* should be memorized.

Readings

Böckle, Franz, ed., *Social Message of the Gospels* (New York: Paulist Press, 1968), Concilium Series, Vol. 35.

Curran, Charles E., *Christian Morality Today* (Notre Dame, Ind.: Fides, 1966).

Dunphy, William (ed.), *The New Morality: Continuity and Discontinuity* (New York: Herder & Herder, 1967).

Häring, Bernard, C.Ss.R., *Christian Renewal in a Changing World* (New York: Desclee, 1964).

Monden, Louis, S.J., *Sin, Liberty and Law* (New York: Sheed & Ward, 1965).

Oraison, Marc, *Morality For Our Time* (Garden City, N. Y.: Doubleday, 1968).

Rahner, Karl, S.J., *The Christian of the Future* (New York: Herder & Herder, 1967).

Theological Studies, June, 1967: "Introduction to the Theological Background of the New Morality," John G. Milhaven and David J. Casey, S.J.; "Situation Ethics and Objective Morality," Louis Dupre; and, "Tension, Morality, and Birth Control," Peter Chirico, S.S.

Understanding the Signs of the Times, Concilium No. 25 (New York: Paulist Press, 1967).

War, Poverty, Freedom: the Christian Response, Concilium No. 15 (New York: Paulist Press, 1966).

SIN

Unfortunately sin is still with us. And it is going to stay. As long as we remain free beings sin will remain a fact of life.

The continuance of sin and the understanding of sin are two different things, however. Traditional thought on the nature of sin is being wholly recast today. This is especially the case with original sin; and personal sin, too, both mortal and venial, is being looked at in a new light. Thus, though sin remains a constant, its explanation is definitely changing.

Original Sin

Few points of Catholic Doctrine seem so well understood as original sin. There are many reasons for this. For one thing, it is usually presented in the concrete imagery of the paradise story. For another, it is always explained as affecting everyone by the mere fact of their being born.

What seems to be a well understood doctrine is, however, under analysis, not well understood at all. This at least is the opinion of several outstanding contemporary theologians. They feel that the Church's grasp of this most complex and fundamental of human tragedies is not only inadequate but to some extent even childish.

Their seriousness on the point derives in part from the challenges raised by modern science and in part from the advantages now enjoyed for understanding the sources upon which the traditional explanation rests. On both scores they feel that the prevailing notion of original sin is capable of significant and beneficial alteration.

Writers like Karl Rahner, Piet Smulders, and Piet Schoonenberg think definitely that a theology of original sin has to consider the data of modern science. The historical sciences, they note, have practically rebutted the idea of mankind's origin from a single couple. The social and psychological sciences, for their part, are convinced that external influences are more formative of persons than internal and even inherited ones.

In light of this these theologians have begun *tentatively* to reshape the theology of original sin. Beginning with the Bible they note that its pages say little or nothing about the actual process by which original sin is passed on. Though St. Augustine thought this process was that of human generation and inheritance, all that the Scriptures affirm is that all men are in sin and, thus, in need of Christ. If anything, the Bible stresses the fact of personal sin as the basis of this need.

These writers also note that the Scriptures give but a sketchy description of what men lost with original sin. It has not been so with traditional theology: the loss of such gifts as sanctifying grace, immortality, integrity, infused knowledge, and inability to suffer has been neatly and consistently recounted.

By way of contrast, modern theologians observe that the Scriptures do not say whether the gifts in question were actually possessed as fully developed realities or as mere possibilities which would have developed had men remained faithful. They also note a trend among early eastern theologians to see these gifts as possibilities.

Turning to statements of the Church, especially to the Councils of Carthage, Orange, and Trent, these theologians find nothing to discourage a recasting of the traditional theology. Again they see a stress laid on the fact of original sin rather than on the process of its transmission. They see nothing to prevent thinking that this process may be more external than previously thought, more social and evolutionary than internal and inherited.

Piet Schoonenberg is probably the most advanced thinker in this vein. He equates original sin with what he calls the "sin of the world." By this he means the complex web of egoistic relationships and institutions that self-centered and unloving human beings have spun around themselves to such an extent that it touches and inevitably engulfs every person.

Schoonenberg spends little time considering the origin of this state of affairs. He presupposes that it began with mankind's first generation, and insinuates that it grew out of man's original moral condition. He infers that though in grace the first human beings were not wholly developed in the possibilities that grace implies. They did not possess such gifts as traditional theology says they did, but only the possibility of these gifts gradually taking form in their being. They were able freely to contradict such moral light as they had, and this they did.

From such a beginning the circle of sinfulness spread ever wider, sin begetting sin. Gradually its extension and intensity became such as to suffocate every human person with the exception of Mary. Others in the beginning may have escaped it, but only because they accepted the grace God continually offered. By the time of Christ's death, Schoonenberg thinks, the web of sinfulness had become so tight as to leave escape impossible.

In speaking of the inevitability of every person's falling, Schoonenberg is not claiming any radical loss of freedom in men. He is at pains to avoid any "totally depraved" notion of human nature. His point is simply one of diminishing moral strength in persons continually subjected to selfish surroundings.

Lacking the possibilities of life that stem from grace, each person is ultimately helpless before the influence of his sinful surroundings. Personal sin invariably follows as a sign of a person's succumbing to the sinful world built by men.

It is with personal sin, then, that original sin finally makes its lethal invasion into the soul of the individual. Each person becomes individually guilty through a personal act of adding to the sinful situation about him.

Baptism equips a child with those inner possibilities that make resisting the "sin of the world" a real likelihood; without them a person does not stand a chance against the web of original sin. In the case of an adult, baptism also frees the person from the guilt of having at one time or another cast his lot with man's sin-filled society.

Personal Sin

Turning to personal sin, contemporary theologians tend to move in the exact opposite direction of their studies on original sin. What they emphasize here is the internal and subjective elements of sin rather than those that are external and objective.

In recent centuries personal sin was mainly analyzed in terms of external acts. Little attention was paid the inner-life of the one sinning. Awareness and consent were presupposed for real sin, but the nature of these was only abstractly examined; actually little was known of their real nature. Of main concern was the degree of prohibition set against certain acts.

Theologians today find this line of thought incomplete. For the most part — there are some notable exceptions — they tend to accept as valid the traditional speculations on how acts are prohibited. They think, though, that forbidden acts are only part of the picture. To see sin fully they stress the relationship between forbidden acts and the inner-life of the one sinning.

Only if a person has achieved such psychological, moral, and even religious development as to be able to give himself totally and with complete freedom to an act seriously prohibited, they say, can one speak of personal mortal sin. Lacking this, there can only be venial sin, which is a decision of one insufficiently mature or self-possessed to make a complete self-donation in that decision.

These theologians think, then, that sin follows the line of a person's inner maturing and spiritual development. Infants, they say, are incapable of mortal sin since they lack the personal and religious maturity to give themselves totally to an act contrary to God. Seldom will even youngsters possess such stature. As for adults, the requisite maturity should also be proved rather than presumed.

Seen in this light a forbidden act may or may not signify a corresponding degree of personal involvement. It may be a sign of a person's complete abandoning of God's will. It may also be a symptom of something entirely different. Each act must be examined separately.

It would be wholly to misunderstand these theologians were the impression to be seriously entertained that they are advocating a certain casualness about either the possibility or fact of personal sin. They are completely serious about the reality of sin. The point they make is that there is more to that reality than has been previously understood. In light of this they are willing to conjecture that mortal sin may well be not so frequently met with as the traditional theology has thought, and that venial sin may well be more serious. But this is a far cry from insinuating that sin is of little significance. At their hands sin becomes even more significant. Being more personal, it is more deeply damaging.

Degrees of Sin

Contemporary theologians see personal sin as admitting of three distinct degrees. Following the tradition, they name two of these venial and mortal sin, but the third, which the tradition called "final impenitence," they call "sin unto death."

What they stress with respect to the latter is that it alone designates personal sin in the strictest and fullest sense of the word. "Sin unto death" is *ultimate* sin; and unless we understand this, they say, we will never understand sin in its other real but less drastic degrees. It is from ultimate sin that we derive both the meaning and nature of mortal and venial sin.

Ultimate sin means "lasting" sin, personal serious sin that is never forgiven because forgiveness is deliberately never asked for. It is "final impenitence" in relation to the moment of physical death, but as a personal state of enduring alienation or divorce from God it can arise and last long years before actual death.

Ultimate sin is what the gospels call the "sin against the Holy Spirit," and what St. Paul calls "iniquity" and "wickedness." It was St. John (1 Jn 5:16–17) who coined the name "sin unto death" for it. It is sin in its fullest and therefore worst form, a "hardening" in sin, a complete and unalterable turning away from God.

Mortal sin, on the other hand, is "estranging" sin, denoting a deliberate discontinuance of the saving relationship with God that is the state of grace. Dreadfully serious, mortal sin is a personal catastrophe: it manifests a personal decision selfishly to stand in being wholly for oneself.

It does not, however, mark the same irrevocable rejecting of God as does ultimate sin. One in mortal sin is not "lost" or "dead" in the same sense as one in ultimate sin. He remains vulnerable to God's forgiving advances.

All things being equal, the mortal sinner remains conditioned for repentance. His sin does not so ravage his goodwill and basic humility as to make him hopelessly locked in selfishness.

Though estranged from God, his state of soul is such as to leave practical hope of an eventual reconciliation.

With every deliberate delay of repentance, however, his condition worsens, tending to develop ever more directly into that of one who has sinned "unto death." And the same is to be said of every repetition of his sin.

With *venial* sin the matter of reconciliation does not even arise. Venial sin is "desensitizing" sin. It denotes a neglect of personal attentiveness to one's relationship with God. It is "hurting" sin rather than "estranging" or "divorcing" sin.

Venial sin issues from an attitude of forgetfulness or oversight. It bespeaks a growing indifference, a loss of interest, and a mood of taking things for granted. It is conscious unresponsiveness in what makes for growth, enthusiasm, and selflessness in one's relationship with God.

Like mortal sin, venial sin, when unrepented or frequently repeated, lays a condition for what is worse than itself. It erodes one's defenses against mortal sin. As such it is the first step in a process whose ultimate achievement is hell. It is a "cooling" of heart whose direct line of growth is eventual hatred of even the thought of God's forgiveness.

Sin's Social Side

In any of its degrees personal sin damages the Church and the world. This point, so seldom treated in the individual-centered theology of recent centuries, is stressed in contemporary theology.

Ultimate and mortal sin wholly smother in a person that selflessness which radiates the goodness of Christ, even when the sinful act in question is not a glaring crime against one's neighbor. Venial sin, for its part, dulls the luster of that goodness. In differing degrees of disability, one in sin is simply not in condition for providing the Christian services his situation may at any time require.

Venial sin deserves special attention on this score. It is not enough that one be good: one must always be better. To neglect expanding one's selflessness is to stifle one's powers of love. The result is to deprive others in any number of ways of what they could otherwise have hoped from a participant in Christ.

Readings

De Rosa, Peter, *Christ and Original Sin* (Milwaukee: Bruce, 1967).

Monden, Louis, S.J., *Sin, Liberty, and Law* (New York: Sheed & Ward, 1965).

Oraison, Marc, *et al.*, *Sin*, transl. by B. Murchland & R. Meyerpeter (New York: Macmillan, 1962).

Regnier, J., *What Is Sin?* (Westminster, Md.: Newman Press, 1961).

Rondet, Henri, S.J., *The Theology of Sin* (Notre Dame, Ind.: Fides, 1960).

Schoonenberg, Piet, *Man and Sin* (South Bend, Ind.: University of Notre Dame Press, 1965).

U. S. Catholic, August, 1967—Special Issue on Sin.

PART SIX

Common Forms of Sin

SELFISHNESS

With its talent for scientific analysis, recent theology unwittingly
bred an understanding of charity as but one among the many
ingredients of Christian living. Charity became displaced from
the center of every Christian expression to the fringe, as it
were, of Christian initiative. Charity became an isolated project
that one was free to concentrate on or not, as obedience or
humility, or the several other Christian attitudes became subjects
of selected endeavor. The synthesis of the Christian life-style
became unraveled. Charity was no longer the heart of the matter
in every Christian expression. Charity became the subject of an
independent treatise, with principles, norms, and checks and
balances, all with little or no vital connection with other areas
of Christian effort.

Drawing its inspiration from Scripture rather than reason,
contemporary theology aims at correcting this "dissected" view
of the Christian life. Charity is again presented as the basic
impulse that gives Christian character to every Christian expression. It is understood as itself the Christian life-style, the
variety of Christian attitudes and responsibilities being but
manifestations of this one essential and unifying impulse.

If this contemporary understanding has any relation to the
view of recent theology, it is in the serious application of traditional "ascetical" theology to the Christian life of everyone. As
charity came to be regarded in recent centuries as the heart
of Christian perfection for those who freely chose to seek Christian perfection, so it is seen today as the fundamental vocation
of every Christian, to be brought to fullness by everyone and
to animate every Christian effort. As a consequence the artificial
distinction between moral and ascetical theology has been "liqui-

dated," and moral theology today simply devotes itself to a study of the love-life of the children of God.

Charity

If there is anything typical of what Christ asks of all who would share in him, it is an attitude of "unconditionality." We have already seen this in regard to *Faith*, and it was implied under both *Law* and *Grace*. Here it need but be stressed that the Lord's injunction to "love as I have loved," and to be "entirely good as your heavenly Father is entirely good," was addressed to everyone and implies a call to set no limits to one's responsiveness. To be a Christian is to announce oneself before God and men as one committed to loving without measure.

In the face of this it becomes inexact to forge a distinction between Christ's commandments and his recommendations or counsels. Recent theology made the latter a matter of choice, defining the *obligation* to love almost entirely in terms of what falls under the Ten Commandments. Contemporary theology regards this understanding of the matter dreadfully defective.

Jesus calls all, rather, to an unconditioned willingness to love in the pattern of his heavenly Father and himself. Christian love takes only initial, not consummate, expression in those responsibilities that denote the minimum fulfillment of God's purposes. Over and beyond this minimum is the whole area of bringing the imitating of God to bear on one's every decision.

The counsels of the Lord rest on all; they are illustrations of what one might do in particular instances if one senses that such would be practical and possible ways of really imitating the Master. They do not, however, represent every possibility. They are examples drawn from Jesus' own life-situation simply to illustrate what he was really driving at. In the life-situation of his followers countless instances of unconditioned loving arise that have no reference at all to Jesus' life and times.

Jesus, for example, said nothing about taking an aisle seat in a bus rather than a window seat. He said nothing about letting others read the morning newspaper first or select the evening's television show. What he said, in word and example, was that one who is truly "in him" must be ready to love in every circumstance without measure. And he illustrated some possible forms this might take: turning the other cheek when struck, giving one in need not only one's coat but even the shirt off one's back, settling a legal conflict out of court, etc. The heart of the matter, though, is that his followers be willing to respond to God's will not only in fundamental and important things, but in everything, giving themselves both toward God and others in that same fullness of generosity that Jesus manifested.

Not everything that Jesus recommended, of course, was meant for everyone. Rudolph Schnackenburg is very clear in his discussion of New Testament morality that some of the practices advocated by Jesus as signs of unconditioned love-willingness presuppose a special grace, a special vocation. Here one should place such practices as vowing poverty or chastity or giving oneself exclusively to the service of the Church. The underlying point brought out by this is that imitating the Lord — answering his call — requires in practice a personal searching of each situation for that manner of self-expression or behavior that really corresponds to life in the Holy Spirit.

As the recent tradition gave rise to "minimalism," so contemporary theology could conceivably give rise to an undue and unrealistic "maximalism," which is another way of saying scrupulosity. The last thing contemporary thought is driving at is unreasonable "obligationism." One is *obliged* to do only what one clearly perceives to be practically possible; one fails the "call of the hour" only when one clearly knows that the only motive one has for not doing what one could do in the name of Christ is unmistakably a selfish one.

There can be countless good reasons why one will not do in a particular setting what might have the appearance of the "better thing." What alone is required is that the reason one actually settles on be as far as possible an expression of one's willingness to act here and now in the manner of Christ. If one fails, he simply repents, without anxiety, and resolves to try better the next time.

Selfishness: a Habit of Mind

It is one thing to treat casually an isolated act of undue self-preference and quite another to be casual about a consistent mentality of self-preference. The latter is well deserving of worry and warrants not a little attention.

Usually the attitude of selfishness is the result of spiritual immaturity rather than fault. Everyone has to be concerned about his own well-being, and one of the very real expressions of charity is precisely this concern. On the other hand, unless self-preoccupation is tempered by the impulse of charity toward others it can easily become a matter of spiritual deficiency.

In the case of youth, self-preoccupation is a kind of developmental hazard. Until inner identity is achieved and a life-purpose determined, youth is highly vulnerable to desires and dreams centering on itself. For all its expressions of glowing idealism — a point not to be dismissed lightly with respect to charity — youth is a time of intense subjectivity.

In our own culture this vulnerability of youth to self-centered phantasy is heightened. Young people are continually exposed, through magazines, television, and movies, to an adult world of life-styles and achievements. Commercial advertising is specifically geared to self-centeredness. Lacking the psychological background to keep self-seeking in context — adults often have this same deficiency — the young are thus continually in a turmoil of wants and frustrations. It is a most difficult period of life, and adults can be thankful they do not have to go through it again. By the same token, they should be understanding and helpful.

Conditioned by all this, the young are prone to reserve prime time for dreaming. "Encroachments" on their time and thoughts are thus strongly resented. They also are easy victims of an urge to expect services that stem from the long developed charity habits of their parents and other adults. Great stock is also placed on "appearances"; things have to be the way they are "supposed to be" or young people have no interest. Often the most selfless and generous offerings are passed off as "phony" because they do not measure up to youth's imaginary standards. Life tends to be defined in terms of themselves, and few if any things outside their limited horizon of values are given serious consideration.

What this adds up to is that the young have a great deal going against them in terms of Christian selflessness. Winning their release from self-centeredness is no small accomplishment, and it is not a victory that will take place without help, often firmly given.

Educating Unto Charity

Two things go into this helping process: a living context to the contrary, and a concentrating on youth's inherent idealism. The first consists mainly of example, the second in guidance.

One can hardly expect participants in a community to manifest a moral and religious level beyond that of the community itself. Except that the young are surrounded by people truly given to perfecting charity in their own lives, one cannot rightly raise a complaint against their self-centeredness.

The devotion of parents to fullness of life "in Christ," taking expression in genuine love between themselves, in services generously offered and kindly accepted, in consistent reverence for things of real value, in a tempering of their own desire for material things, will be of untold influence as a day-by-day formative force.

Correcting the selfishness of their children will also be part of this love-service, which often will be more effective the more it suggests concrete possibilities to the contrary. Emphasis, in other words, should not be on what not to do, but on what the children might positively do to be less taken up with themselves.

The latter point deals with what ideally should be the heart of parental teaching and guidance with respect to charity. Everyone wants to be respected and appreciated, young people no less than adults. Everyone wants to be good, and to be recognized as such. Awakened to the thought, the young want to be "lovers" of the most accomplished kind. Keeping before their minds the manifold opportunities for loving those around them can only confirm this "lover" instinct. Suggesting and planning instances of generosity toward others, both within and outside the family, should be a great part of parental teaching. More effective yet will be inviting young people themselves creatively to suggest and plan in this way: in this case charity will be coming from within them, which is the end always to be sought.

Selfishness as Sin

Though often the product of immaturity, selfishness is also the product of deliberate unwillingness to sacrifice oneself in a situation calling for generosity in the Spirit of Christ. In such instances selfishness is sinful, possibly even seriously so.

It is easy to see that selfishness is the heart of mortal sin. What is not so obvious, what is not sufficiently adverted to, is that selfishness is also the central impulse of venial sin. It is this latter point that deserves more attention. All the eroding effects of venial sin stem from selfishness, and these spell misfortune not only for the individual person but for the entire Church.

Fundamentally, selfishness is a failure to answer to the basic movement of grace: life befitting one fashioned in the Spirit of Christ. Psychologically it is an attitude that blocks the unconditioned quality characteristic of genuine Christian activity. It is the setting of limits to the extent one is willing to love. Correspondingly it denotes a stunting of relationship with Christ and others, a curtailment of development in that relationship.

The particular malice of selfishness is especially evident when viewed in relation to life in the Church. Selfishness in this context is the failure to express social or fraternal care, an attitude always inconsistent with the Spirit of Christ, and at times even contradictory of that Spirit. It implies a turning away and in some instances a betrayal of the service-call of the Christian state. Selfishness is a personal blocking of the impulse of fraternal love and responsibility.

Rather than building community, therefore, the selfish person wills to stand in isolation. He breaks down community, not only because he sets limits to his contribution to those with whom he shares life or because he refuses any contribution, but also because his self-preference usually brings in its wake irritation and reprisal on the part of others. The selfish person gives scandal, provoking others either to follow his example or to injure charity by way of retaliation.

Isolated acts of selfishness are one thing and a pervading attitude of selfishness quite another. The former can be quickly repented and more easily corrected. The latter, however, is

less easy to get at both by the person himself and those desirous
of his healing. From it, moreover, issues a multiplicity of un-
Christian actions and reactions. Even as a product of immaturity
and defective moral training, it induces a kind of blindness
to one's surroundings, especially to the possibilities of charity
that daily occur. When reinforced by habits of approving decisions, one is not only blind to possibilities, but stands even with
a hard heart against those opportunities for charity that are
seen. Selfishness grieves and restrains the Spirit; left unhealed
it can suffocate every breath of genuine love.

Readings

Gilleman, Gerard, S.J., *The Primacy of Charity in Moral Theology*
    (Westminster, Md.: Newman, 1961).
Häring, Bernard, C.Ss.R., *The Law of Christ* (Westminster, Md.:
    Newman, 1961), Vol. 1, Chap. 6, pp. 300 ff., and Chap. 9, pp.
    350 ff.
Schnackenburg, Rudolph, *The Moral Teaching of the New Testa-
    ment* (New York: Herder & Herder, 1965), Part 1, Chap. 3; and
    Part 2, Chap. 2.
Schoonenberg, Piet, *Man and Sin* (South Bend, Ind.: University of
    Notre Dame Press, 1965), "Results of Sin — Inability to Love,"
    pp. 70–79.

DISOBEDIENCE

Recent and contemporary theology are in full accord regarding the nature of law, obedience, and disobedience, but they differ with respect to their practice. Contemporary theology insists that legislating, for example, must always be done in relation to the real personal goals of a community or individual. Obedience is understood as both an attitude and an act of "collegial" responsibility, whether for the community's or one's own well-being. And disobedience is distinguished into that which is irresponsible and that which is responsible, the latter being but obedience to that for which laws and precepts are themselves supposed to exist.

In all of this contemporary theology is but setting the recent theology of obedience and disobedience in a broader and more adequate context. It introduces few elements not to be found in the classical synthesis, but places these elements in more balanced relationship. What results is an approach to obedience and disobedience that is personal rather than mechanistic, moral rather than legalistic, theological rather than ethical.

Fundamental Notions

Of primary importance is the realization that legislating for human well-being must always be done with reference to the genuine personal goals of a community or individual. In the Church this means that laws are to be made with a view to bringing the faithful to the fullest possible sharing of the mystery of Christ. Civil laws have as their objective the fullest possible temporal well-being of the civic community, understanding well-being here not so much in materialistic as personal terms: happiness, peace, freedom, participation, self-determination, etc. Personal precepts, for their part, have meaning only in relation to the moral maturing of the individual.

In all these cases legislating is for the sake of persons and authentic personal life. None deal wholly with mere physical accomplishment, as do, for example, military orders and game rules. In the Church especially the mere manipulating of persons or situations has no place whatever, though the same is true of the state and home. To lose sight of the personal purpose of legislating is to run the danger of claiming for laws an "absolute" character that they simply do not possess.

A second thing to be noted is that laws exist for the personal well-being of a community. Their purpose is to support and guide the whole community in pursuit of its personal goals. They lay claim to the obedience of the individual insofar as he is a participant in the community and thus shares responsibility for the community's achieving its purposes. Precepts, on the other hand, are directives imposed specifically on individuals. Parental decisions often take the form of precepts. These have as their objective the supporting, instructing, or correcting of an individual, and bind in conscience no less than laws.

Determining whether laws and precepts really fulfill personal purposes is the responsibility not only of legislators, but of the community and individuals as well. Contemporary theologians see in obedience an element of responsible evaluation regarding what one is commanded to do. Obedience is not merely an act of conformity to a legislated norm, but an act of responsibility for a community's or an individual's real well-being. Responsibility for personal goals, therefore, is a "collegial" enterprise, shared in, in due measure, by legislators and subjects alike.

Obedience

Though one decides freely to obey, just laws and precepts actually lay a prior claim to this decision. Just laws and precepts restrict freedom in that they point to an objective that one is freely to pursue. Obedience is precisely the free acceptance of this restriction.

Obedience to laws is sacrificing self-interest to community-interest. It bespeaks, therefore, commitment to community values. Though having meaning as an achievement of one's own well-being, by contributing to the achievement of the community's well-being in which one participates, obedience to laws has fuller meaning in being a service to a community. And this should be its chief motive.

Among the many values of obedience, therefore, especially where laws are concerned, is the community-centeredness it reinforces in a person's spirit, and the deepening of selflessness that this implies. Theologically examined, obedience to laws has still richer values. It can be seen, for example, both to signify and bring about a sharing in the humility of Christ, who for the sake of others subjected himself fully to the human order, including mere legalities. This sharing is, in turn, a growth of participation in Christ's mission to offer perfect praise to the Father, and to further the salvation of men. Since God bequeaths his saving love most directly, clearly, and abundantly in and through what is in harmony with faith and reason, obedience either promotes or restores a situation in which this saving love abounds.

What has been said of the meaning and value of obedience to laws holds also, but in a different way, for obedience to precepts. Here one sacrifices self-determination to meaningful guidance. The benefit of this is that one becomes thereby a more capable participant in the community. By securing personal well-being, by refining one's sense of responsibility, obedience to precepts indirectly conditions one for sharing in the values of obedience to laws.

Educating For Obedience

Moral maturity is a matter of reaching a state of steadfast self-commitment to what is of real worth for personal and community well-being. This maturity is the goal of all moral education, and it must be specifically the goal of forming persons in obedience.

Laws and precepts have their sole value in pointing persons toward what is truly for their well-being. Similarly, obedience must always be taught in such a way as to lead persons beyond mere compliance to directives to a personal devotion for the good with which the directives are concerned.

Laws and precepts support human freedom, which is ever

prone to spend itself, out of weakness, on what does not pertain to genuine life. They must never be allowed to suffocate or replace freedom, however, by calling undue attention to themselves. Overmuch legislation easily does this. So do arbitrary and autocratic expressions of authority.

Obedience is best taught, therefore, by awakening persons to what is truly good, and supporting their fragile devotion to it by few but wise and firm directives. Rules should be explained, at least to the extent that the good being aimed at is clarified. And they should deal only with such good as cannot be neglected without significant personal loss. Other good should be pursued by way of counsel, if counsel be necessary.

With an eye ever to their purpose, therefore, rules and regulations should have about them an element of self-liquidation. This is particularly the case with precepts devised for individuals. As soon as individuals show signs of pursuing their well-being responsibly, even if not always consistently or in ways "preferred" by those set over them, precepts should be relinquished in favor of responsible freedom and exhortation to an ever higher moral idealism. In the case of wise laws, on the other hand, a community is well-advised to retain these simply for the sake of its weaker members.

Responsible Disobedience

Laws and precepts must always harmonize with true community and personal well-being. They are, in fact, mere human judgments of what is thought suitable or fitting as means for achieving that well-being. There may be many other means of achieving this, and there usually are; laws and precepts represent the selecting of one of these by those in authority.

At times the means selected by authorities is simply inadequate. It works undue hardships; it looks to achieving only a portion of the well-being really possible or perhaps necessary; it leave persons unresponsive to values they should be more attentive to.

Since laws no less than persons are subject to what is truly good, laws and precepts that represent a practical disregard of community or personal well-being simply do not impose a claim on conscience. Commitment and responsibility to the genuine good surpass obligation to laws which themselves fail to embody this commitment.

Reaching this conclusion in a concrete situation requires far more than mere "whim." The act of responsible evaluation that contemporary theologians associate with genuine obedience is a judgment to be arrived at by means of serious examination of the situation at hand. Only cautiously, even reluctantly, is a negative conclusion to be drawn, and only then if the inadequacy of the law in relation to the real well-being of the community can clearly be shown. The more serious the law, moreover, the more shared that conclusion should be in the community.

This happens, though, more frequently than people are generally accustomed to think. And one does not have to appeal to laws that are blatantly unjust to illustrate this. Laws that remain imposed long after the situation inspiring them has passed are an example. An undue multiplication of laws is another. Laws that deal with nonessentials, that seek to change by the fact of legislation wholly indifferent things into what is intimately connected with personal or community well-being, also exemplify this.

To those schooled in recent theology, this casualness about setting limits to the obligation of laws will smack of anarchy. But it does no such thing. Authority is as vulnerable as freedom with respect to the truly good, and little is accomplished by pointing to the weakness of the one and "absolutizing" the other. The spirit of contemporary theology is to take seriously the weakness of both.

Authority and freedom are both subject to what surpasses them in value and for the achievement of which they exist. Authority is as much in need of persons freely committed to the truly good as persons trying to achieve that state of commitment are in need of authority. Human life begs for a continual interplay between the two. As freedom always stands in need of wise directives, so do even wise directives stand in need of responsible evaluation.

Important to note here is the difference between being obliged in obedience to adequate laws and being obliged in charity not to disrupt the unity and peace of a community faced with inadequate legislation. Obedience and charitable conformity are wholly different things; and their difference should not be forgotten, especially in an era of renewal.

Obedience presupposes good legislation, good in the sense of aiming at genuine well-being. Responsible disobedience, on the other hand, presupposes that charity does not require conformity for the sake of unity and peace. Rarely does charity call for aggressive disregard of conformity, especially where the problem is that of inadequate rather than unjust legislation. Seldom does it call even for passive nonconformity, though such a call is surely at times issued. Charity achieves its goal, usually, by a patient and creative bearing of a bad situation; but never should this procedure be called obedience.

To admit that laws and precepts, by reason of defects, do not oblige does not at all pose the threat of anarchy. What it threatens is that real values will be taken more seriously than inadequate directives. Anarchy, which is an irresponsible reaction to responsible authority, results only where participants in a community have not been educated in obedience beyond the point of mere legal conformity. Neither is anarchy sufficiently prevented by an understanding or practice of legalities that refuses to persons the right of responsible evaluation. Surely some of the "authority crisis" of today is a "backlash" from a situation such as this. What alone prevents anarchy is devotion to genuine human and Christian values; and this devotion is obedience in the fullest sense of the word.

To be sure, authority bequeaths to a directive a certain primacy as a means to achieving genuine well-being. And this will not be lost on one devoted to the value aimed at by the directive. Real obedience is an honoring of this primacy; and it is a practical honoring in that obedience means sacrificing personal freedom regarding the selecting of another means to the same value.

By the same token, however, this primacy arises not so much from the decision of one in authority as from the adequacy of the means itself. Authoritative choices do not change inadequate means to well-being into adequate ones. Neither does theology support every decision made by authorities, no matter how inadequate. What theology supports is that inadequate legislation bespeaks the weakness of men, and, except that commitment in charity to higher values urges otherwise, this weakness is to be patiently borne for the love of Christ. Again, though, charity and patience are not obedience, and never will be.

Irresponsible Disobedience

Deliberately to disregard responsible directives aimed at the achieving of genuine well-being is to engage in irresponsible disobedience. Its malice, when disregarding laws, consists in betraying a community's claim to one's pursuit of the community's well-being. In the case of disregarding personal precepts, its malice is that of substituting self-assertion for commitment to genuine value. Underlying both is the malice of disregarding the well-being to be achieved for the sake of determining for oneself the means to its achievement.

Ultimately irresponsible disobedience entails the loss of genuine well-being, whether partially or wholly, depending on its seriousness, since it is no longer being sought on its own terms. One cannot demand moral or spiritual goodness; one cannot tyrannize growth in the Spirit. This can only be achieved by selfless pursuit; as Gerald Vann has said, one can only woo goodness. One who disobeys attempts to determine the course of his own fulfillment, and he is always the loser.

Especially to be noted is that disobedience lessens or even cancels participation in a community's well-being. Disobedience is a particularly distasteful version of selfishness. One chooses to act at the expense of others, denying them a service of support to which they have a right. Achieving a community's well-being requires the selfless contributions of all. The disobedient person declares himself an exception to this, setting his own course without gratitude or concern toward others.

Readings

Häring, Bernard, C.Ss.R., *Law of Christ* (Westminster, Md.: Newman, 1961), Vol. 1, Chaps. 4–5.
——— *The Liberty of the Children of God* (New York: Alba House, 1966).
McKenzie, John L., S.J., *Authority in the Church* (New York: Sheed & Ward, 1966).

UNCHASTITY

Recent and contemporary theologians teach the same thing in the area of sexual morality outside of marriage but from wholly different perspectives. Reduced to the simplest terms the difference is that the one group was mainly negative while the other is wholesomely positive. For all practical purposes the evaluation of irresponsible sexuality by the unmarried is identical with both schools of thought. The manner of lessening or controlling its occurrence, however, and above all of developing a sense of sexual responsibility differs greatly.

Friendship and Chastity

I have often wondered what would indeed result if we converted the massive efforts of our dating code into a vast educational program of self-knowledge and the dynamics of personal, responsible love. It is unfortunate that we have armed our charges with such precise distinctions in matters of sex and have spoken to them so little of the nature of friendship. Perhaps, we did not know about the love of friendship ourselves.

One does not have to subscribe to all the complaining of Father James Kavanaugh to see sense in what he is saying here. He makes the point well that chastity will best be understood and best develop in a framework of friendship.

The truth of this is seen from both the nature of human sexuality and the nature of marriage. Except that human sexuality be the manifestation of two persons bonded in total and irrevocable love it is the enacting of a lie. Except that marriage be a state of friendship, with sexuality at the service of love, it too is a fraud.

Outside of marriage the case is not otherwise; it is, in fact, more acute. Sexual indulgence here is more obviously a saying in the flesh of something other than what is being said in the spirit. The body is used wholly or intimately while the heart is evidently reserved. The sign surpasses the statement.

In the case of persons not at all in love the lie implicit in shared or forced sexuality is, of course, monstrous; their act is nakedly barbaric. Friends at least are more humane: the very fact of friendship insures for sexual indulgence at least the semblance of love-making. The defect is in the quality of their friendship. Were it more genuine it would be a barrier against fraud: it would prompt only what is in harmony with their real but necessarily restricted love.

Friendship, then, is a key to chastity. It excels mere prohibitions by focusing the partners on their real well-being. At the same time it fulfills prohibitions by disclosing unchastity for what it really is: an injuring of love.

Except for friendship a person can never love, and an ability to love is the heart and soul of chastity. The importance of parental friendship toward their children cannot be exaggerated. Upon it depends a child's root sense of self-worth. Without it a child is set against the world, a condition of spirit that will manifest itself in all kinds of aggressive and defensive behavior throughout his life.

Happily, a child can escape the impact of this default if someone else along the line takes time to help him experience his own worth. In the process, though, he is likely, time and again, to turn against himself in "isolated" unchastity. This will probably occur even in a context where a child has been loved from the beginning, but in this situation it will be far less symptomatic of difficulty and more easily corrected. Parental and other adult friendship toward a child is the greatest and perhaps only bulwark against solitary unchastity.

Family friendship is also the great security against undue sexual indulgence in the particular relationships that begin during adolescence and early adulthood. All too often these relationships and their unfortunate degrees of intimacy are subconscious substitutes for what should have been the young persons' heritage since birth. One cannot carry on friendship with due measure who has never had a due measure of friendship.

Unchastity in youthful and irresponsible adult relationships issues also from a defect in approaching a love affair positively and creatively. Persons are customarily schooled to curb their love energies rather than direct them. All is well, they are taught, as long as certain boundaries are not trespassed.

But romance is a job, a task, within the scope of one's broader life-project. It is not at all simply doing what comes naturally over and above the observance of a few prohibitions. A love relationship that is to lead anywhere in terms of personal development and purpose has to be *created*. It is something that has to be taken hold of and directed along calculated lines. And the lines are human, Christian, and personal.

To be sure, there is a negative aspect to this. Persons must be prepared to withstand what threatens their relationship-project. But even though it be true that "love without power is not enough," as Robert Johann, S.J., has commented in favor of prohibitions, the "power" in question must first be a force of commitment to what a relationship can accomplish rather than avoid.

The Christian Dimension

In the case of Christian friends, both this force of commitment and the possibilities of their relationship have a distinctive flavor. Chastity, which is a feature of this force of commitment, is essentially a holding of the relationship in fidelity to the life-style required of those sharing in Christ. It is the energy of love motivated and directed by life "in Christ." Its specific object is revering the personal quality of sex "in the name of the Father," and so managing the relationship that it will enhance rather than lessen the worth of that quality.

Christian persons should be led to see friendship as a sharing of *charity*. What bonds them together is far more than the "mysterious affinities" of human affection. The underlying power of their union is the oneness of Spirit born of Christ's healing and creative love for them.

And the attitude issuing from this, a very reproduction of Christ's own heart and mind, is that of deepest commitment to one's own and the other's "ultimate dignity." Christian friendship is precisely for the sake of bringing the partners to fullness of maturity as children of the heavenly Father. It is precisely for the sake of what charity is all about, but, being friendship, it is a situation wherein charity can take form so much more fully and understandably than elsewhere.

The great value of Christian friendship is precisely this ability to illustrate charity, to disclose and embody it with a clarity surpassing all its other manifestations. Christian friendship, thus, must be seen as a "service" to be accorded others: it presents to their gaze some hint of what Christlike love for all is to be like.

Sinfulness of Unchastity

Leading people to this vision is the main burden of contemporary theology's message on sexuality. It is also the basis of its analysis of the sinfulness of unchastity outside of marriage. And herein it stands in glaring contrast to recent theology. The latter, by regrettable but unintended oversight, stressed only prohibitions and the degrees of malice corresponding to the seriousness of these prohibitions. Contemporary theologians place the classical prohibitions in a fuller Christian context, and temper their malice by a practical rather than idealistic person-centeredness.

The first point of contrast concerns "solitary" unchastity. Contemporary theologians are becoming ever more reserved regarding concluding to serious sin in this act. For the most part they are satisfied that the tradition is correct in seeing self-abuse or masturbation as a serious disorder. Surely they hold "to a man" that it is something a person is gradually to win freedom from. But they are willing to emphasize the gradual character of this liberation, and by that very fact see more in its continuance than bad will. Bad will, in fact, seldom if ever has anything at all to do with it.

Thus, the general mood of theorists and practitioners today is to take seriously the probability of lack of full freedom in this disorder. Rarely will self-abuse, especially among the young, be certainly an instance of reversing one's commitment to God. The law of confession before communion if one be in mortal sin will consequently rarely come into play. By the same token, contrition for such personal involvement as the act indicates is of special importance, since liberation from this impulse of the flesh, for all that friendship can help, must be won from within — and it must be won. Critical, therefore, is not so much the recurrence of the act as the recurrence of one's commitment to rid oneself, by positive goodness, of its sway.

As for shared sexuality outside of marriage, whether it involve the complete sharing of bodies or merely undue intimacies, recent and contemporary theology differ not at all as to its prohibited character. The person-centeredness of contemporary theologians leads them to evaluate incidents of this kind within the framework of love straining for maturity, and they are thus disposed to be generous in applying the traditional — and sound — principles regarding occasions of sin.

No reputable theologian, however, has been led by this generosity to suggest that sexual acts have a due and honored place outside of marriage. The very person-centered meaning of sexuality, which is the contribution of modern philosophers and theologians, places its expressions apart from marriage on even stronger grounds of prohibition than does the procreation meaning contributed by the tradition. Not that it is worse to lie than to have an illegitimate baby. The disorder is that an act having procreative meaning, or even gestures of a kind normally associated with such an act, bears human and Christian purpose only when signifying total and irrevocable mutual responsibility.

Unchastity in the unmarried continues to be evaluated within the framework of the traditional teaching that its fully deliberate expression, whether in terms of intercourse or undue intimacies, is a serious disorder. Bernard Häring, a leading contemporary moralist, has suggested, and on this he would be supported by the many theologians who are rethinking the nature of serious sin, that instances of light sexual stimulation, even when deliberate, may normally be of insufficient consequence to be mortally sinful. They can be, when made a sign of one's willingness completely to ignore his relationship with God, but this would be exceptional.

There seems to be a strong element of common sense in this suggestion, but whether it be acceptable or not to the community of theologians remains to be seen. What is certain for now is that those who are unmarried must gradually win freedom from all sexual disorder in their relationships. If this process be furthered by regarding many of their mistakes as only lightly wrong, then let them be so regarded. What seems of greater significance is that the process itself be continuing forward.

Immodesty

To be immodest is irresponsibly to endanger one's own or another's commitment to revering in charity the mystery of sex. And this is wrong, in the judgment both of traditional and contemporary theology.

Because modesty is the extension of chastity to what even threatens a lessening of the charity-commitment regarding sex, modesty is the finest achievement of chaste love. It deserves to be cultivated diligently, and few things among the many gifts of Christ surpass in delicacy the charm it adds to a personality or relationship. Nothing makes a friendship so secure in goodness and potential as modesty.

Modesty cannot be instilled by insisting on conformity to relative standards, whether of dress styles, ways of dancing, kinds of books to read or movies to see. Neither does putting certain parts of the body and gestures of affection "off limits" do the trick. These help, of course, and sound directives are needed both to begin the process and support its continuance. As often as not, though, they are obstructive of the process, since those who formulate them fail to stay awake to their essentially relative character. Threats to chastity, with which practical directives are to be concerned, do not remain constant. Even St. Alphonsus, whom many misunderstand as the severest of moralists, was remarkably generous when it came to acknowledging that custom lessens danger.

Modesty is a *personal* regard, a cherishing, of what enhances chastity. It is an inner attitude or posture, not an external conformity. The malice of immodesty is precisely an inner disregard of chastity's vulnerability, not a physical disregard of some preprogrammed norm.

The developing of modesty therefore requires positive direction toward what nurtures chaste love and friendship. Modesty is not so much an "avoiding" force, as a creative force: it aims at building a situation wherein the treasure of sexuality is secure and enriched. Directives about modesty should have about them, therefore, an element of self-liquidation as the creative process of modesty takes hold. Modesty comes only from within, and more than other virtues, adjusts to the real and changing world.

Unlike chastity, which deals with a constant, namely, sexuality, modesty bespeaks a person managing himself "in Christ" amid things that change. There is nothing constant about the way modesty takes expression: what it forbids in one setting as dangerous it allows in another because danger is not present; what it discourages one day for the sake of security it encourages on another day for the same reason. Immodesty, on the other hand, belies a desire to do what one wants without any sensitivity to the day or setting, above all without any regard to the vulnerability of others.

Modesty in girls and women is the chief indicator of the moral level of a culture. Where girls and women are possessed of regard for sex, where they are solicitous for the vulnerability of boys and men with respect to sex, all can be well. Modesty and immodesty in their case hinge on their commitment to temper "in Christ" both their feminine self-centeredness and fascination for fads.

With boys and men, on the other hand, modesty and immodesty hinge on a willingness to keep things in context. Psychologically, boys and men are prone with respect to sex to see only the part, not the whole. They must be led always to keep sex in its real personal setting. To be moved by persons rather than "charms" is their gain from modesty — which is another way of saying that modesty insures love, both for boys and men and for girls and women.

Readings

Bertocci, Peter, *Sex, Love, and the Person* (New York: Sheed & Ward, 1967).
Buckley, Joseph, *Christian Design For Sex* (Chicago: Fides, 1952).
Häring, Bernard, C.Ss.R., *The Law of Christ*, (Westminster, Md.: Newman, 1966), Vol. 3, Chap. 4.
Johann, Robert, S.J., "Love Is Not Enough," *America*, October 9, 1965, p. 404.
Nedoncelle, Maurice, *Love and the Person* (New York: Sheed & Ward, 1966).
Oraison, Marc, *Learning to Love* (New York: Hawthorn, 1965).

GROWTH

From our own inner experiences we can often derive insights for an understanding of external movements and trends in which we are participants. This is especially true of the inner experience of personal and religious growth. From it can be drawn fruitful analogies for both understanding and participating in the changes that mark the life of the Church in our time.

Our inner life, if examined closely, is a dynamic thing, the continuing movement of which is toward personal and religious maturity. So, too, the life of the Church, especially those features of it with which the preceding pages have been concerned, is dynamic, a movement toward fullness of understanding and mission. From personal growth, therefore, we can derive some understanding of doctrinal growth. Doctrinal growth, in turn, suggests an understanding of the especially significant aspect of the Church's growth today commonly called the ecumenical movement. In all this, again, we meet the historical or process element in human experiences, even in those that are typically Christian.

Personal Growth

Father Louis Monden, in his excellent little book, *Sin, Liberty and Law*, has described the process of Christian growth according to three stages of personal maturing. Though hardly a new idea — it is found in the spiritual theology of the medieval monks, and is hinted at even in the Book of Sirach's teaching that the fear of God is the beginning, fullness, and crown of wisdom (Sir 1:9–18) — Monden's presentation is enriched by the conclusions of modern psychology.

During infancy, he explains, we take on the basic "cut" of our personal spirit. The experiences which a child undergoes serve to give the child the particular "stamp" of responsiveness that will mark its personality for life. Not that the child is unable to change as it grows. Rather, *what* will have to be changed, if that be necessary, is now established.

Arriving at adulthood, therefore, we find ourselves moving along a particular line of emotional responsiveness. We may be fundamentally secure or insecure. We may be predominantly selfish or unselfish. We may be given to deep and many attachments, or relatively indifferent. All of this is in great part a carry-over from childhood experiences.

Adulthood also finds us confronted with the prospects of managing our own affairs, which is mainly a matter of having to make responsible decisions. We have to direct ourselves now toward goals of our own selecting. Life can no longer be mainly a process of automatic response to what is happening in and around us.

Faced with adult challenges and possibilities we find ourselves either assisted or hindered by those habits of responsiveness that carry over from childhood. Some of these habits or patterns we find distinctly helpful toward pursuing adult goals; others we experience as having to be modified or removed if we are ever to achieve those goals.

Maturing, then, is an opening of ourselves to adult values and ridding ourselves of those patterns of responsiveness which, though they served our childish needs, serve now only to close us to what deserves to be loved and cherished simply for its own sake.

There is more to adult life than what is naturally fulfilling, however. There are greater goals than those which reason alone honors. There is a Christian perspective to adulthood that calls for a still higher openness and more complete responsiveness.

Religious maturing, in other words, is, according to Father Monden, the high point of personal maturing. And this again involves a process of opening ourselves to new values and ridding ourselves of what prevents their being either appreciated or pursued. Impediments in this case, however, are as much the self-induced preferences of adulthood as those carried over from our youth.

Religious maturing involves readjusting patterns of responsiveness that have been deliberately developed. As many of the automatic responses developed in childhood do not serve adult living, so many responses deliberately developed during adulthood can be of little advantage when it comes to religious and especially Christian maturing.

A true openness to life in Christ and the Church requires a unique freedom from the limited openness of self-concern, noble though that self-concern may be. It also requires a level of responsiveness that reaches even to total self-sacrifice. Gradually to free ourselves of what restricts both our awareness of Christian values and our freedom for responding to them is the central labor of personal Christian maturing.

Doctrinal Growth in the Church

Extending this to the life of the Church as a whole, the same truth, the same process, can be seen both verified and required. Refining awareness of Christian values and releasing freedom for responding to them are the central task of the Church's growth.

Accepting this assertion presupposes, of course, that one understands the Church as something historically dynamic, as something that is meant to grow. The chief inspiration of "new" theology is precisely this understanding. Were the Church not a living thing, a community of human beings gradually unfolding in the fullness of Christ, a "new" theology would be a waste of time. So, too, though, would have been the "old" theology, since it was also an aspect of a process. As it attempted to formulate the awareness of the Church in a former day, and to remove entrenched restrictions to the Church's freedom for response to what she was thus made aware of, so "new" theology is attempting now. Who rightly understands the Church and her doctrines will easily perceive this.

Many, though, do not have this correct understanding, and for them the "new" theology is a real distress. Growth in the Church has not been a feature of the instruction they received, and all too often continue to receive. This "static" outlook, seemingly of such value in recent centuries, is of a sudden one of the great disservices to the Church. Those possessed of it, those who have enshrined it in their mind and spirit, must gently but firmly be guided out of it. At least opportunities for their release must be offered. For them or their guides to turn away negligently from this "call of the hour" is to forfeit the maturing of the Church. Maturing in the Church is very similar to personal maturing; if the process is refused, the havoc and suffering of immaturity inevitably result.

The Ecumenical Movement

A glaring instance of damaging immaturity is the continuing disunity of the Christian Churches. Entrenched in attitudes and feelings appropriate to a former day, and still on a grand scale both unable and unwilling to see that both the Church and its problems change with growth, the Churches remain fundamentally isolated rather than gathered in the maturing process of unifying relationship.

To be sure, much has been done, even a miraculous amount, in recent decades. And rare is the Church that has not been wholesomely touched by the current ecumenical trend. The process is slow, however, and in relation to what has actually to be achieved, has hardly begun. What retards and impedes it is in great part a blindness or resistance to the notion of growth.

Countless Christians, be they Roman Catholic, Protestant, or Orthodox, continue to experience the disunity of the Christian Churches solely as an historical problem. And their discussions of it, if they discuss it at all, whether among themselves or with their separated brethren, feature an historical perspective.

Catholics of this mind see only that Protestants disrupted the unity of Christianity, severed themselves from the one true Church in the process, and have thus to "return" to Rome if the problem is to be solved; and much the same attitude is extended toward the Orthodox. Protestants, on the other hand, see only a betrayal of the Gospel by Roman "institutionalism," especially with its emphasis on ecclesiastical authority and alleged apostolic traditions; only a wholesale "reform" of the Roman Church, doctrinal and pastoral, gives any hope of an eventual solution, and even then the solution will never be a "return." The Orthodox, for their part, see only the grievances suffered by their medieval forebears at the hands of a power-usurping Roman Church; the apologies of Rome and a complete liquidation of the pseudo-primacy of the Roman Pontiff can alone heal the breach.

What is missed in all this is the "real" ecumenical problem. The real problem is not an historical one at all, for all that it has an historical aspect. It is a problem of the here and now. The very posing of the ecumenical question requires a lifting of the separated Churches out of their past context and seeing them as they are at this time.

The ecumenical question is stated in different ways. A contemporary Lutheran theologian, Carl Braaten, has recently stated it thus: can the Protestant reform movement long justify its continuing existence in the face of a reformed post-Vatican II Roman Church? Others put the question in this way: how do you *re-establish* unity among the Christian Churches, or how *reunite* separated Christians? Far less polished, but still to be met with among Catholics even of an ecumenical bent, is the more traditional form: how do you bring about a *return* of the separated brethren to the true Church of Christ?

None of these questions seem to reach the heart of the matter. All more or less carry over into the real issue an obsolete historical perspective, and to that extent both cloud and clutter the real issue. The real ecumenical question has to be drawn purely from the facts at hand: real Churches, populated by real people, professing to be real Christian communities, yet co-existing in real separation or disunity. And there are further facts: all the Churches are long removed from their historical origins, and their true relationship today has grown out of a continuing shifting of their historical separation. The situation facing them is not that of the eleventh or sixteenth century, nor that of any of the intervening centuries, but that of today.

The ecumenical question seems better posed, therefore, as this: how simply to *unify* the many Christian Churches in such a way that they can *be* the one Church of Christ. Free of such notions as "reunion," "return," and "reform," this phrasing of the question brings Christians directly into contact with the real problem, namely, *unity*. And it envisions the only real solution: that the Churches *be* the one Church of Christ, not "become," "discover," or "re-establish" that one Church. Phrased with a view both to the Roman Catholic Church's belief in her own identity and to the shared conviction of *all* the Churches that they are communities "in Christ," this statement of the ecumenical question concentrates entirely on what the Christian Churches must do in order to be together in fullness what they all are in fact but in isolation. It also points the Churches' energies in the only direction that a solution can be found — in the future, and it implies a key to the one way of bringing about that future solution.

This statement of the ecumenical question, with its implied advantages, is drawn mainly from Protestant sources, from a symposium of Protestant theologians reacting to Carl Braaten's version of that question. Sifting their thoughts, one finds an understanding that the Christian Churches confront each other today laden with both genuine and ungenuine Christian elements. Each brings to the encounter positive commitments to the gospel and negative reactions to the commitments of one another. Each must discover, whether by humble soul-searching in isolation or by humble dialogue with one another, which of their commitments and reactions are truly authentic in the light of the Christian sources. Each must be prepared to retain what is genuine and to forego what is not. And as Braaten has observed, with the unanimous acceptance of his reactors, solving the ecumenical problem may be accomplished only if all these divergent lines move toward a synthesis that will incorporate what is genuine in each.

Approached on this level, the ecumenical problem is not at all a battle to be won, but a task to be accomplished. It is a task, moreover, that has to be shouldered by more people, which will happen only if more begin actually to "feel" the problem. The continuing disunity of the Christian Churches simply must not be allowed. If the urgency of the issue, and especially its "future" rather than historical aspect, were to be taken more personally by more Christians surely something would happen.

If the Roman Church's energies of orthodoxy, for example, and the Protestant Churches' energies of reform were to be turned on the living issue, rather than on that which originally set them apart, surely these energies could be channeled more creatively and beneficially, even more quickly, toward the envisioned future synthesis. If the sympathies of the Orthodox could be directed more to the tragedy of a disunited Christianity than to their own historical grievances, they too could make an unforgettable and wholly necessary contribution. Our greatest deficiency is that we too often aim our energies at what is neither the real ecumenical issue nor the real direction of its solution.

As the real issue has been the product of growth, so its real solution depends on growth. And here again we meet the necessary process of maturing, in the sense of a willingness to disengage oneself from what is a carry-over from past feelings or decisions, and to adjust oneself creatively to new demands and situations. What is so true of persons is here seen to be true of Churches. If their disunity is to be healed, they must mature.

And what is true of the Protestant and Orthodox Churches is just as true of the Roman Catholic Church. In fact, the call to maturity imposed by the times on the latter is even more pressing. Only if Roman Catholics, who celebrate themselves before the world as possessors of or participants in the one true Church of Christ, are willing humbly to evaluate their own commitments and reactions can this be expected of those who have never made such a universal claim. Only if Catholics are willing to endure the painful process of doctrinal maturing can they expect the same of their separated brethren. Only if all are willing to grow in spirit and theology can the necessary and long-overdue synthesis ever take place.

Readings

Abbott & Gallagher (eds.), *Decree on Ecumenism,* in *The Documents of Vatican II* (New York: Guild Press, 1966).

Baum, Gregory, O.S.A., "The Ecclesial Reality of the Other Churches," *Concilium* No. 4 (New York: Paulist Press, 1965).

Bea, Augustine Cardinal, *et al., Peace Among Christians* (New York: Herder & Herder, 1967).

Braaten, Carl E., "Rome, Reformation, and Reunion," *Una Sancta,* Vol. 23, # 2.

———— "Rome, Reformation, and Reunion — A Symposium," articles by Albert C. Outler, Warren A. Quanbeck, George A. Linbeck, Robert McAfee Brown, and Carl E. Braaten, *Una Sancta,* Vol. 23, # 3.

Congar, Yves, O.P., *Ecumenism and the Future of the Church* (Chicago: Priory Press, 1967).

Häring, Bernard, C.Ss.R., *Christian Maturity* (New York: Herder & Herder, 1967).

Monden, Louis, S.J., *Sin, Liberty, and Law* (New York: Sheed & Ward, 1965).

Theology Digest, Winter, 1967 — Special Ecumenical Issue.

Index